ALSO BY REEVE LINDBERGH

Under a Wing: A Memoir

The Names of the Mountains

The View from the Kingdom: A New England Album
(with Richard Brown)

Moving to the Country

Reeve Lindbergh

No More Words

A Journal of My Mother, Anne Morrow Lindbergh

Simon & Schuster Paperbacks
New York   London   Toronto   Sydney

Simon & Schuster Paperbacks
Rockefeller Center
1230 Avenue of the Americas
New York, NY 10020

Copyright © 2001 by Reeve Lindbergh
All rights reserved, including the right
of reproduction in whole or in part in any form.

SIMON & SCHUSTER PAPERBACKS and colophon are registered
trademarks of Simon & Schuster, Inc.

For information about special discounts for bulk purchases,
please contact Simon & Schuster Special Sales at
1-800-456-6798 or business@simonandschuster.com.

Designed by Deirdre C. Amthor

Manufactured in the United States of America

3   5   7   9   10   8   6   4   2

The Library of Congress has cataloged
the hardcover edition as follows:
Lindbergh, Reeve.
No more words: a journal of my mother,
Anne Morrow Lindbergh / Reeve Lindbergh.
p.   cm.
1. Lindbergh, Anne Morrow, 1906—Last years.   2. Aging parents—
Family relationships—United States.   3. Authors, American—20th century—
Biography.   4. Women air pilots—United States—Biography.
5. Parent and adult child—United States.   6. Mothers and daughters—United
States.   7. Lindbergh, Reeve—Family.   I. Title.
PS3523.I516   Z76   2001   818'.5209—dc21   [B]   2001049196

ISBN-13: 978-0-7432-0313-5
ISBN-10:   0-7432-0313-5
ISBN-13: 978-0-7432-0314-2 (Pbk)
ISBN-10:   0-7432-0314-3 (Pbk)

For my mother,
with love beyond words

Acknowledgments

I would like to thank all those who helped to make this last period of my mother's life not only possible but also remarkable: a time of care and comfort and laughter and joy, even in the daunting presence of frailty, confusion, anxiety, and ill health. Thanks first of all to my brothers, Jon, Land, and Scott Lindbergh, and to their families, for their unceasing patience and understanding, their wise counsel, and for visiting us often, traveling over great distances and in all kinds of weather in order to be with our mother at frequent intervals throughout the year.

Thanks to my beloved husband, Nat Tripp; to our son, Ben; to Nat's sons, Eli and Sam Tripp; and to his mother, Alice W. Tripp; to my daughters, Elizabeth and Susannah Brown; and to our niece and nephew, Connie Feydy and Marek Sapieyevski, who have willingly and uncomplainingly embraced my mother's care and well-being as part of their own lives, for many years.

Thanks to all our neighbors, relatives, and friends in Vermont, in Connecticut, and around the world for their loyal affection and attention during the past decade of my mother's life and mine. Thanks to the doctors, financial and legal advisers, and health care professionals and organizations who steadfastly supported our efforts to care for her at home during an increasingly vulnerable and fragile old age.

Special thanks to Ann Cason and to the "Circle of Care" she gathered around us during my mother's last months here in Vermont. The following people generously offered my family the unique and ongoing gift of themselves. Whether they provided daily personal care or organized occasional musical gatherings, whether it was a doctor or dentist arriving at the house to check on her at the end of a busy professional day, or a stylist coming over the bumpy dirt road to give her a new hairstyle and manicure once a week, whether the visitor was a woman of her own age, driven by her daughter for afternoon tea, or a neighbor's three-year-old coming for a ten-minute visit on a gloomy afternoon, each of these people enriched my mother's days immeasurably, as they did mine. I am so grateful to each of them:

Ann Cason
Susan Drommond
Alexandra Evans and
    Phil Sentner
Buncie Shadden
Carla Leftwich
Laurie Crosby
Catherine Clark
Catherine Thomas and
    Rhoda Thomas
Trudy Meuton
Sue Gilman
Susan Shaw
Karen Frazier
Lillian and Mia Concordia
Jim and Sherri Lowe

Harold Turner and Jane
    Fuller
Marco Alonso and Ruth
    Taylor
Ted Soares
Janet and Rick White
Dr. Tim Thompson
Dr. Fred Silloway
Laura, David, and Bea Brody
Newcomb and Ditty
    Greenleaf
Carol and Patton Hyman
Arthur Jennings
Trenny Burgess
Sherlyn Morrisette

⤳ 𝄞

The poetry and prose excerpts that I've included in this book are drawn from the following sources: *Gift from the Sea, The Unicorn and Other Poems* by Anne Morrow Lindbergh; "Disillusions of Childhood," "Distance Lends Enchantment," and "Success" from *The Wheel* (Miss Chapin's School), March 1924; "Caprice," "Letter with a Foreign Stamp," and "To ———," from *The Smith College Monthly* in the October 1926, February 1927, and May 1927 issues, respectively; *Local Vertical* by Anne Spencer Lindbergh; *Autobiography of Values* by Charles A. Lindbergh, and *Four Quartets* by T. S. Eliot.

I also used excerpts from some of my mother's unpublished notes, and have referred to, though not quoted from, several other books during the course of keeping my journal, including *The Illuminated Rumi,* translated by Coleman Barks; *The Little Book of Prayers,* edited by David Schiller; *Living Buddha, Living Christ,* by Thich Nhat Hanh; *The Essential Rilke,* selected and translated by Galway Kinnell and Hannah Liebmann; *In Every Tiny Grain of Sand, A Child's Book of Prayers and Praise,* collected by Reeve Lindbergh.

Now there are no more words,
But you will know, when I sing
For others, that I bring
To you alone
A leaf, a flower, and a stone.

—Anne Morrow Lindbergh, from
  "A Leaf, a Flower, and a Stone,"
  The Unicorn and Other Poems

Preface

These pages represent a kind of journal, with chapters taken from my own diary entries, written off and on between May 1999, the time my mother came to live with us in Vermont, and February 7, 2001, when she died. I first began to keep a record of this period for myself alone, hoping to make some sense of my turbulent thoughts, feelings, and moods surrounding my mother's presence and care. I realized that in some ways my own inner world was as scattered and as volatile as hers seemed to be, in our final months together. And, like my mother before me, I knew that the only solution for me in a time of such difficulty and confusion was to write. This is not, however, an exact reproduction of my diary. It became clear to me as I continued writing that I was writing a book, and that I was writing it in the hope that what I revealed of my own experience, as honestly as I could, might help other people in similar family situations. I found myself expanding upon the original entries as I typed them into the computer, adding a new thought here or an old memory there, as these thoughts and memories came to me.

I also chose to use excerpts from my mother's writings as

chapter headings and to incorporate some of these in the body of the book. It was very important to me that her writing voice, too, should be heard in this record of events that concern her so deeply.

She was not able to write about the last part of her life in the way that she chronicled so much of her earlier experience, with candor, skill, and eloquence, for more than sixty years. And she will never read what has been written here about her. All the same, the truth about this book is that it is not mine but ours.

Summer 1999

My mother is ninety-three now, an age she never expected nor wished to achieve. She has outlived her husband, her two sisters, her brother, one of her sons, one of her daughters, and two of her grandchildren. Ten years ago she experienced a series of strokes and was left physically frail and confused, which resulted in the need for full-time care. With round-the-clock caregivers to attend her, she continued to live in her home in Connecticut. Someone, either a caregiver or a family member, would drive her north to visit me and my family in Vermont, where she has a house on our farm, for weeklong visits several times a year, and for holidays.

On Memorial Day weekend 1999, Mother was diagnosed with pneumonia here in Vermont, and since then she has not been back to Connecticut. Even before this happened, my brothers and I felt that our mother had become too isolated in her home. Her circle of old friends was fast diminishing, and her neighbors, who remained loving and loyal visitors, were beginning to be concerned about her. It had become very difficult for her four children to monitor her well-being from the distance of our own adult lives in other parts of the world. We decided that it was best for our mother to stay with me in Vermont for the time being.

Mother does not live in my house, but in a smaller one that my husband, Nat Tripp, designed and had built for her just up the dirt road, only a hundred yards away. I visit her in the evenings, but full-time caregivers keep her company twenty-four hours a day. They help her eat and dress, and tend to her bathing and personal care. Most of them are Buddhists, associated with a Buddhist meditation center established in Barnet, Vermont, in the same year I moved to the area. The head of the team is Ann Cason, who has been a Buddhist as well as a care professional—a coordinator of care—for more than thirty years, working all over the country. I met Ann when she created a care system for my uncle John Wilkie in New York during his last years. His widow, my aunt Margot, a lifetime Buddhist, has been one of my mother's closest friends for seventy years. My mother, who is not a Buddhist, used to describe herself as "a lapsed Presbyterian," but Aunt Margot still referred us to Ann Cason.

I know that Mother is very fortunate to be able to afford such care, and that I am very fortunate to have her near—but not in—my home. All the same, I don't know what to do with her. It is the silence. It isn't a matter of not being able to talk to her. I can talk, but she doesn't answer, though I believe that she understands everything I say, even if she chooses to pay less attention at certain times than at others. She rarely answers, in fact she rarely speaks, and she does not write at all. This astonishes me. Words were central to her life for as long as I have known her, and yet she appears perfectly comfortable without them. She does not miss them. I, on the other hand, am at a loss. I am bewildered, confused, absolutely at sea, in my mother's silence.

1

September 1999

I learned to know the world through words, but they were not my own. From the beginning of my life, as I remember it, everything I understood was made plain to me in her language, which I knew much better than my own. Her quiet voice, her exquisite gentle articulation, her loving eloquence, all of these things spoke me through my days, comforted my nights, and gave each hour of every twenty-four its substance, shape, and meaning from the time that I was born.

She knew me well, and at each moment of my need, she spoke the words I needed. Sometimes the words were abstract, the language vague, but the message was always uncannily the right one for that instant. When I was a child—the youngest of her five offspring—and injured or unhappy, she would say, "Everybody loves you, Reeve!" and that was enough to draw the healing circle of affection around me and mend my trouble, whether it was a skinned knee or a bruised heart.

When I was grown and had my own daughter, and reveled in the ecstatic connection between me as nursing mother and my baby at my breast, my mother watched us and told me, "It is, of course, the only perfect human relationship." This made me laugh, but at the same time, I believed her. I still do.

Then later, when I lost my first son just before his second birthday, she who had also lost her first son knew what to say, and she was one of the few people I was willing to listen to. She told me the truth first. After I had found my baby's dead body one January morning, just after it was taken away but before the family had gathered together in shock and bewilderment to comfort one another, my mother said, "This horror will fade, I can promise you that. The horror fades. The sadness, though, is different. The sadness remains . . ."

That, too, was correct. The horror faded. I left it behind me in that terrible winter, but the sadness remained. Gradually, over the years, it became a member of my family, like our old dog sleeping in the corners. I got used to my sadness, and I developed a kind of affection for it. I still have conversations with it on cloudy days. Come here, sadness, I say, come sit with me and keep me company. We've known each other for a long time, and we have nothing to fear from each other. But my mother was right. It does remain.

At the time of my son's death, when I asked my mother what would happen to me as the mother of the child, how that part of me would continue, she said, "It doesn't. You die, that's all. That part of you dies with him. And then, amazingly, you are reborn."

At the time, it was very hard to believe the last part of what she said, although I understood the dying part. It felt that way, certainly. I did not expect to feel any other way, ever again. But she was right again. I died with my first son, and then later, never thinking it could happen, I was reborn into a whole different life with my second.

Sometimes I still hear my mother's voice in my head, telling me that all is well, that the logic of existence is intact—not painless but intact and, in its own way, beautiful—and that she is still here.

In fact, she is still here. And she speaks on rare occasions, but not in the clear, quiet voice I used to know so well, inhabited by a meaning intended, as I always believed, just for me. One of my mother's great gifts with language was that each person who listened to her, like each person who read her books, believed that she was talking intimately and exclusively to him or her.

Age and illness have silenced her now, and she lives in silence to such a degree that speech, when it does come, seems unfamiliar to her, her voice hoarse and thick with the difficulty brought on by disuse, a rustiness of pipes and joints too long unlubricated by their once normal flow. She speaks to make a discomfort known, perhaps—"I'm cold"—or to ask an idle question: "Is someone in the kitchen?" "What are you reading?"

Reading. There it is. Reading. That's where I have learned to look for her lately. That's where she is. That is where she *lives* now. Reading. I am just beginning to understand, and my understanding excites me in the way an explorer must feel when coming to the top of what seemed an impenetrable mountain, treeless with rocky escarpments and no view, and suddenly, without warning or expectation, sees a whole new country beyond . . . fields, forest, a river that was not on any map.

She once conversed and kept silence only briefly, as an emphasis in conversation. Silence for her was like a rest in music: a pause with a point. She would stop talking, then sigh, then look me in the eye or glance briefly, mysteriously away. Then she would say something that would make me laugh, or that I would write down to treasure always:

"Grandmothers are either tired . . . or lonely!" "The cure for loneliness is solitude." (I am just beginning to understand what this means.)

Later, poignantly, after my father—along with most of the men of his generation—had passed away, she would tell me, "Grandchildren are the love affair of old age." When we asked a friend to design and paint a toy chest for the grandchildren who visited her, we had that aphorism painted on the side of it.

Now, instead of conversing, she reads. She reads almost constantly, unless she is sleeping, or eating, or watching a video on television in the evening. She often reads without interruption; even when company is in the room, she does not look up from the book, sometimes for hours.

She reads while sitting in the armchair in her living room, from any one of a pile of books neatly stacked on the table in front of her, near the vase of flowers, and the collection of smooth stones, a seashell or two, and one stuffed plush robin that was given to her as a party favor at a grandson's birthday in July. It's a Beanie Baby, I notice.

"I love him very much," she says to me, when I pick up and hold the stuffed bird for a moment, admiring his puffed-out red breast and the brightness of the two plastic yellow-and-black beads that are his eyes. Does she remember the party? Does she remember the grandson? (The last time my brother Land called, when I was sitting with her, she told him, "I'm here with my sister," and looked over pleasantly at me.)

I don't know what she remembers, and I finally have learned not to ask. In any case, it would be rude to interrupt her. She is reading.

Sometimes, if I am with her for several hours and she leaves the room to take a nap or to use the bathroom, I look through the pile on her table to see which books she has chosen for the week. The first time I did this, I almost laughed out loud—not at the reading material, but at my own surprise.

These were the same books, or at least the same authors, I had seen for forty-five years on her tables and shelves. There were even some of the same titles I had memorized as a child, without understanding their meaning, when I lay on the bed in her room early in the morning, after having crept into bed with my parents in the middle of the night because of a bad dream, or a sudden noise outside, or simply because I had fallen into one of the unnameable bottomless crevasses of fear and loneliness in which some children find themselves when there is darkness everywhere.

Here they were all over again: *The Divine Milieu* by Pierre Teilhard de Chardin; *Four Quartets* by T. S. Eliot; Rainer Maria Rilke's *Duino Elegies*. I remembered these all so well. I remembered, too, as I looked at the *Duino Elegies* how many years it took before I could appreciate Rilke, despite having been introduced to his books on my mother's shelves almost before I could read. The air was so thin as to be almost un-breathable, it seemed to me, in the intellectual and poetic at-mosphere in which this man lived and thought. His literary and poetic presence was so ethereal, so romantic, that I couldn't imagine him in the flesh and could not picture him with any physical body at all.

As a teenager, I was taken by my mother, who adored Rilke, to the church where he was buried in a village in the Rhone Valley in Switzerland. There I was told that the poet had died from an infection caused, my mother told me in a voice hushed with awe and sorrow, "from the prick of a rose . . ." All I could do at the time was nod respectfully, but inside I was muttering to myself, *Give me a break!*

I came to love Rilke despite his lofty aesthetics, and I should not have been surprised to see him so well represented in my mother's daily readings. Why was I so surprised? Was it that her reading sophistication was so much more elevated than her conversation level? Isn't that true for all of us? Most people can read much more profoundly than they can write, speak, or even think. For me, this is one of the great humiliations of being literate at all. If I can read Shakespeare, why can't I write Shakespeare? It's not fair.

I suppose I am surprised that my mother's ability to read and think has not been taken from her, while the ability to use what she is reading and thinking clearly has. Or has it?

I make so many assumptions in my love for this person who is very old and very quiet. Desperate for communication, equally desperate for some kind of certainty in the bafflement and enigma that her old age has presented, I hang on every one of the few words my mother utters. I decide at certain moments that my aging parent has always been an oracle. At other moments, depressed and discouraged, I think she must have become an idiot.

I rediscovered a printed copy of a speech she delivered in New York City in 1981, about aging (she was then seventy-five), and I found it so moving that I brought it to show her last week, and to read it aloud, in the evening. She had spoken to a group of women at the Cosmopolitan Club about the inevitability of moving from stage to stage in one's life, and the need to welcome each stage with a different readiness while learning from the movement itself. She likened the process to a game of musical chairs, and she quoted Simone Weil, T. S. Eliot, Bernard Baruch, and others. At the end of the speech she read from one of Eliot's *Four Quartets*, "Dry Salvages," finishing with these words:

The moments of happiness—not the sense of well-being,
Fruition, fulfillment, security or affection,
Or even a very good dinner, but the sudden illumination—
We had the experience but missed the meaning,
And approach to the meaning restores the experience
In a different form, beyond any meaning
We can assign to happiness.

My mother's caregivers loved the speech as much as I did. "Thank you, Mrs. Lindbergh," someone said into the quiet after I finished reading. "Those are wonderful words."

"Aren't they?" I said. I was pleased and turned to my mother in her chair. "It is such a beautiful speech—so much insight, so much humor. It's a gift!"

But my mother was looking at me with an intensity that I had misinterpreted. She had looked this way all through my reading, and I had thought it was a listener's intensity. Instead it was internal preoccupation, something with too much force of its own to allow her to hear anything else. "Take me!" she said. "Take me away! They spank children here!"

I don't think there was a pause. We all reassured her at once. *Nobody* would spank her, nobody spanked anybody here.

"I don't allow spanking on my farm!" I said with a smile. We all talked about spanking among ourselves—all except my mother, who had fallen silent once more. I recalled, to the room in general, my mother's fear of one grim childhood nanny. Had she been spanked far, far in the past? It must have been awful.

"They spank children!" my mother said several times, as if she hadn't heard the conversation at all. We continued to reassure her until finally she said to me, as if weary of the whole topic, and of me and my lack of comprehension, "Please— go." It was late, and I went.

Into the pool of mystery—which frightens me—leaps a whole team of explanations, like lifeguards, busily rescuing me with their practiced phrases: "She doesn't understand what she's saying . . . This can't mean anything. It's just non- sense." Or, conversely, "What is she trying to say? It must mean something very important. I must try to understand. What's wrong with me, that I don't understand?"

Conversation was so integral to my own sense of my mother's life and identity that I cannot accept its absence. I find myself inventing her speech when I am with her, and con- tinuing with the invention long afterward. Now my mother's eloquence has found new life in my mind, and in my dreams.

I dreamed that we were together on a bench at a railway sta- tion. All three of us sat there: first me at one end, then right next to me the mother I had known all my life—vivid, elo- quent, well dressed—then at the far end, this little silent one, only half visible. That is to say, she was not fully fleshed but ghostlike, a human being already partly vanished into the ele- ments. She was pale gray and insubstantial, a fog-person.

"You just have to take care of her," my real mother said to me. She was authentic, I knew. Her voice was clear and com- pelling, her eyes that dark blue I knew so well. She was wear- ing a trim suit and a traveling hat (the one false note; she never wore hats) with an improbable feather poking out the back of it, jaunty and unusual, an inch wide but a foot long. It looked like a pheasant's feather. This made sense because my mother has always been fond of pheasants and had a particu- lar favorite she used to feed on her lawn in Connecticut. But the hat itself was very uncharacteristic. Perhaps I should have felt warned, but I did not. I was comforted.

Her voice was so welcome! It was absolutely familiar. I had
not heard it, or that tone in it, for so long. It was her teacher's
voice, gentle and insistent. She was telling me a truth I could
not doubt. She was giving me an instruction.

"You just have to take care of her, Reeve. Nothing else."

Just take care of her. Nothing else. This I could understand.
This was my real mother's message to me from her real self,
about my task as it related to this vestigial, wraithlike Other
Mother, by whom we were both confronted and crowded on
the railway bench. There wasn't really room for all three of us.
We were uncomfortable as we waited, and I never learned
how many of us were going to get on the train. But my mother
had the answer. Just take care of her. That was all I had to do.
I didn't have to understand her or identify with her. I didn't
even have to love her, as I had so intensely loved my real
mother, for more than fifty years.

How simple, and how wonderful! My mother had returned
to me, and she had healed my hurts and solved my problems
once again.

Long ago, when my infant son Jonathan developed encephalitis, he became unfamiliar to me for a time in the mani-
festations of his disease. He did not seem to be the baby I
knew, cheerful and responsive. Instead he was fretful, racked
with crying, prone to spasms and other strange movements
and behaviors that I had never seen and could not interpret or
control. I was exhausted from his condition and my own. The
long vigil of his illness had left me sleepless. When I did sleep,
I dreamed that my sick child was a changeling. At the end of
the ordeal, the dream told me, if I just had the courage to see it
through, I would get my own boy back. This one would vanish
into whatever eerie dimension he had come from, and my own
beloved healthy infant would return.

I have often felt this way about my mother, in recent years, so it was a joy to find her again in the railway-station dream, just as I always knew her (except for the hat). And with her words, she had lifted my trouble and my burden.

But then, of course, I woke up in the morning and remembered that there is so much else! In a situation like mine, there is memory, and there is frustration, and there is grief, and there is guilt. In fact, there is more guilt than anything else. No matter how good the care provided, no matter how much attention or how much money is spent to address their needs, no matter how extensive the medical treatment lavished upon our beloved elders, there is always guilt, and it is always the same.

We feel guilty because our parents are living at home and are not doing well. We feel guilty because they have been removed from their homes by our arrangement and are not happy about it. We feel guilty because we live far away from them and do not see them often enough. We feel guilty because we live close by and still don't see them often enough. We feel guilty because we live with them and see them every day, but our presence does not seem to help them.

I think we feel guilty about our aging parents, regardless of their circumstances, not because we have *not* done our best for them but because we *have*. Our efforts only emphasize the truth that we and they must live with every day. Whatever we have done, whatever we continue to do, it isn't enough. It won't change the fact that we cannot keep them alive, not forever. We cannot keep them healthy and happy, we cannot keep them with us much longer. They are exactly where they are, close to the end of life. There is nothing we can do about it.

It strikes me as ironic that even though my mother is frail, confused, tired, and nearing the end of her life, she also has to keep moving. She already moved away from her former life— her friends, her work, her routines, even her most familiar daily surroundings, now that she is no longer in her house in Connecticut but in her "vacation house" with me in Vermont.

She left her marriage behind twenty-five years ago when her husband died. After more than forty years of life as half of a partnership, and a complex partnership at that, she moved abruptly into a completely different stage of life, one that she referred to in her writings as "active widowhood." Then, fifteen years after his death, her own health deteriorated suddenly due to a series of small strokes. At that time her life changed even more abruptly than at my father's passing, which had been a relatively gradual process. There was a period of agitation and confusion. The round-the-clock care in her own home, with the accompanying loss of control and independence, must have required an extraordinarily difficult adjustment for her. It may have produced, in itself, some of the agitation from which she suffered, and from which we all suffered at that time.

My own feeling is that she has been restless ever since. Even her reading seems restless, with a quality of seeking, yearning, moving, trying to go somewhere. Something in her now always needs to keep moving, to expend energy on motion, whether of the body, mind, or spirit. Yet at the same time, she appears very tired.

What a disturbance all this movement must be! What agitation and locomotion old age brings! Maybe my mother is simply too travel conscious, too preoccupied by the perpetual journeying, to make conversation. She has no time for anything but the essentials. She is ready to go, dressed for the journey, pheasant feather in her cap, waiting for the train.

On the rare occasions when she talks with me, really talks, using more than one or two words at a time, she often discusses traveling. She speaks with a good deal of urgency, too, as she repeats to me and to her caregivers that she wants to go home. I don't know where "home" is for my mother now. I used to think, since she said this when I was with her in Vermont, that it must mean she wanted to go back to Connecticut, to the house she and my father designed and built in 1963, on the property where they raised us all in a much larger house, which they sold to another young family after we grew up.

My mother lived in this second, smaller Connecticut house for thirty-six years, much longer than in any other home my parents had shared since their marriage in 1929. But her caregivers tell me that when she is in Connecticut, she says then, too, she wants to go home, even more frequently than she says it now in Vermont.

This has me stumped. What does she mean? Is she thinking of the house in Englewood, New Jersey, where she spent her own childhood? Is it some favored one among the many homes she and my father shared all over the world? England, France, Switzerland, Hawaii? Is it an actual home, in the sense of a physical place, at all?

I have theorized that this "going home" was a kind of metaphor, representing my mother's instinctive spiritual urge to leave the body and become united with the vastness of the universe—that my mother, in simple language, was asking to be dead. I'm not so sure about this kind of thinking, though. Is it her wish that she be released from the burden of her aging body and her drifting mind, or is it mine? This is always the question when one tries to interpret the wishes of someone who makes us uncomfortable and who cannot speak for herself. Someone else's silence is a vast field of temptation, an open invitation on which to project one's own conscious or unconscious thoughts.

I remember driving her over a highway in New Hampshire only a year or two ago and being startled to hear her say in a loud voice, after a long silence, "I'm afraid of dying!"

I was moved almost to tears and tried to think of a way to respond sympathetically. Of course she was afraid of dying. She was frail, and weak, and ninety years old.

"Yes, I can certainly understand that, Mother," I offered gently, hoping she would talk further, that the talking might help her with her fear. "But what is it, exactly? Is it the thought of dying itself, a sense of pain and struggle, or is it leaving old friends, leaving the world, leaving your family . . ." I struggled for other examples and felt myself warming up to this discussion, but she looked over at me with irritation and said firmly, from the passenger seat, "It's your *driving!*"

The other night, when she expressed again her unfathomable longing to go home, I tried to respond with understanding and kindness, mixed with solicitude. "Are you sure, Mother? It's very late. Do you really want to get in a car and drive all those hours, all the way to Connecticut?"

She fixed me with a speculative glance. Who was I? What should she say? Then she replied thoughtfully, "Well, I wouldn't mind doing a little shopping on the way."

The evenings with her are not always easy, but they are lively and rich and full of surprises. It is in the mornings that my life is most often a stone in me. I sit crouched and small around it, weighted down at the bottom of the pool that is now murky with questions I cannot answer and responsibilities I don't understand. There is no possibility of surfacing, there are no lifeguards in sight. Again, at these times I don't know whose gravitational pull it is, mine or my mother's that has sunk me so deeply in such unclear waters.

Looking in the morning mirror, I ask myself, *What is that face I see? How did I get here from childhood?* A fifty-four-year-old woman with glasses and wrinkles, brooding about her confused ninety-three-year-old mother in diapers. This is not what I asked for! This is not where I wanted to be!

My mother, at least, is free of numbers, free of the besieging notions we all have about numerical age. A few days ago, on an afternoon when language was flowing more freely for her than usual, a friend of a granddaughter of hers asked her gently how old she was.

"How old am I?" she repeated, as if surprised by the question. Why would anyone want to know?

Someone helpfully prompted, "You just had your ninety-third birthday, isn't that right?" But she looked up, laughed, and denied it. "Heavens, no! I'm about sixty-five." It sounded right. I remember that year. She was working hard, writing introductions to her journals to be published by Harcourt in a series, and my father was still alive. I think he had begun to be ill by then, but the illness seemed peripheral to their lives—a little trouble, as yet undiagnosed.

For myself, every morning the confusion and bewilderment and loss in me moves slowly and lightens as I wake up to the details of the day. "The Good Lord is in the details," someone wrote, and it is true that I rise, through one detail after another, every day. Maybe I rise to meet Him, I don't know. I have no sense of my final destination. I know only that I'm ascending, and that I'll surface eventually, and that details do the job.

First I am lifted, just a bit, by the wet leaves of autumn on the lawn outside my window. Then I continue a little more, watching the old dog who drinks from a puddle in the driveway. I rise further because the puppy has left a puddle on the newspapers in her bedtime crate, because it is not possible to wallow with stones and mysterious pools and clean up after a puppy at the same time.

Coffee and orange juice are always uplifting, and so is sunlight. The kitchen is warm and bright. Soon my husband and my son come down the stairs, one big and gray-haired, one small and tousled, both still blinking with sleep.

Nat is looking for coffee, Ben for his socks. He never says "I can't find my socks," but instead, politely, "Do you know where there might be some socks?" As if his socks were a community household item, like pencils, with many possible and generalized locations.

"There should be some in your top drawer," I suggest, "or else in the laundry basket. Or maybe there's an extra pair right here in the kitchen, in the bag with all your soccer stuff." I get enthusiastic about my suggestions. I rise higher, up from the murk, heading toward the light and perhaps toward the Good Lord, too; triumphantly holding up a pair, in fact many potential pairs from any number of hiding places, of Ben's clean white socks.

Soon we are in the car driving to school, and Ben starts a discussion with me about words.

"When I say 'a few,' Mom, how many does that mean to you?"

"A few? It depends. If you're talking about an audience for a concert, then twenty would be a few. But if you're collecting eggs in the barn . . ."

"Let's say eggs."

"Then I'd say three is a few."

"What about 'a couple'?"

"Two." Two is always a couple to me. I suppose sometimes three could be a couple, if I'm in a sloppy mood. But not when you're talking about eggs. I wouldn't call three eggs a couple, not at this time of year, when the light is dwindling and the hens are holding out on me. In November I'd call three eggs an abundance.

"How about 'a group'?"

"Like a group of people? Maybe five or six. More than three, anyway, but four could qualify as a group, just barely."

"And 'a pack'?"

"Eight, at least. That's my opinion." How many wolves in a pack? How many wolves snapping at my heels throughout life? The wolf of fear, the wolf of sadness, the wolf of death, the wily wolf of love.

"Okay, now 'a crowd.' " Ben is orderly, more interested in progression than rumination.

"Twenty. Where does this come from, Ben?" School? Television? A game somebody else taught him?

"Just from my mind. Hey, what's 'a flight'?" He asks this as we drive up the longest hill, almost a small mountain in New England terms.

"As in birds? A flight of swallows?"

"Sure. Why not?"

We reach the crest of the hill, and suddenly I am all the way awake, my sun has risen. There is open sky above us, autumn trees, branches not quite bare but tattered with leaves, edging the pastures all around. The hillsides, brown and gold, spread downward below us. I am above, flying with Ben's birds.

They are just from his mind, and yet they circle and sweep the sky, a flight of swallows, light as snow or wind or the memory of spring, free of earth and thought.

"At least a dozen," I say, and we're over the top, heading into the valley.

"That makes sense," my son agrees comfortably.

Down the winding valley road, across the bridge and over the short paved lane into the school grounds. As he gets out of the car, Ben is suddenly older, swinging one strap of his backpack over his shoulder. He is in seventh grade this fall. He needs to leave me now and get into his school self and his classroom, but I can't quite let him go.

"Ben, I have just one thing to say to you. Do you know what it is?"

That I love you deeply, that you have floated me up above the surface of the murky mysteries this morning, and then, even further, have helped me to rise up with swallows into the wide and optimistic sky.

He smiles. He knows.

"Mom, I'm already late, almost. See you."

"See you."

We wave at each other, and he walks away. I turn the car around and drive home, wordless, into the opening day.

2

October 1999

The passionate gust that sets one free
—A flock of leaves in sudden flight—
Shatters the bright interior tree
Into a shower of splintered light.

—Anne Morrow Lindbergh, from "Interior Tree,"
  The Unicorn and Other Poems

What I have is a day.

I think I have other things, so many that they spin in my head and churn in my stomach, making me dizzy with a kind of backward self-importance. I think I have myriad responsibilities and burdens, each one distracting me from the others, all of them multiplying so fast that there are more and more in motion around me all the time, like the nightmare of breeding broomsticks in *The Sorcerer's Apprentice.*

I think I have a very old and frail mother who may be dying (but don't bet on it) and whose present life it is my job to watch over and to care for. I also think I have something called a "busy schedule," writing books and traveling in connection with the books, speaking to groups of adults and children around the country. I think I have work to do here on the farm, for my family and the animals: dogs, chickens, sheep, horse, rabbit, not to mention the finch my younger daughter left behind when she moved to California, and Ichabod the lizard, for whom I have the greatest respect because of his apparent serenity. Ichabod lives behind glass, perched quietly on a log in a terrarium by the living room window, almost immobile in his own reptilian world. He shares this place with the constant movement of live crickets, who are at once his companions and his food. He watches the crickets for hours on end, only his eyes and the pulse of his lower jaw moving. Once in a great while he darts out—who would expect this of him, after such concentrated stillness?—and eats one.

Because it is in my own nature to gobble up with a mother's voraciousness everything about my children, I think I have my son's soccer games and dentist appointments and band concerts and even his big feet. (How did those tiny feet I saw for the first time in the delivery room twelve years ago get so huge? I will have to take them shopping for new shoes . . . again.) And on Ben's feet there are his socks, those same white socks that lifted me heavenward one morning last month, and on the rest of him his other clothing, which gets dirty every day. I think I have laundry to do, and dishes to wash, and after that I think I have correspondence piling up unanswered on my desk.

Oh, yes indeed, I am overwhelmed, overloaded, and traveling over my weight limit, dragging with me my treasure chest of daily obligations. I guard them jealously—mine! mine!—I take them with me wherever I go, cling to them so tightly that I am grinding my teeth and hunching my shoulders as I drive over the back roads of northern Vermont this very morning, while on all sides, breathtaking views offer themselves to me one after another, like silent greetings in a language I don't know how to speak, generosity unrecognized in every direction.

I can feel the tightness in my shoulder muscles and make a conscious effort to relax them. I am aware of the struggle inside me and I want to ease up on myself, escape from my own thinking, open my shoulder blades like wings and fly out into the larger atmosphere.

This is the day. In this day there are not only roads and hillsides, trees and light, but there is also sky, and beyond it a whole universe, and how microscopic a piece of it I am, me and my beloved burdens of responsibility. I try to think about the universe, but it is too abstract and too scientific a concept, and it brings a rush of scattered associations: *Star Wars,* Stephen Hawking, astronauts, the Hubble Space Telescope, Leonard Nimoy and Luke Skywalker. My mind is immediately in orbit, accompanied by quantities of space debris. This doesn't help.

I start over again, trying to see beyond myself but maybe not quite so far: a mile or so this time. I look across the valley to a forested hill where all the trees are now bare of their leaves. There is sunlight on the branches, giving a collective lightness and softness to the scene, as if the treetops were feathers or fur and the hill itself a large, sleepy animal warming itself in the morning sun.

I remember flying over these hills with my father in a small airplane in 1972, out of the Berlin airport near Montpelier, where he had rented an airplane at dawn. And I remember floating over the hills again in a hot-air balloon with my sister, Anne, in 1990, on her fiftieth birthday (also my forty-fifth, because we were born the same day, October 2, five years apart).

On both occasions I had the illusion that the trees below me were gentle, the air benevolent. It should be possible to step out and swim in the element through which we moved as safely and as easily as in water or in dreams. I should be able to float down through the feathery treetops and land in their furry arms and come to no harm.

Steady, there, Reeve, daughter of pilots. Fasten your seat belt and curb your imagination. I know there is danger in this kind of sensation when aloft, as in the diver's "rapture of the deep," but I wonder if there is not some more profound molecular truth to it as well. When we are immersed in the enormity of an enveloping element—air, water, space—why would there not be a sense of safety in that immersion, some primeval instinct, deep within ourselves? At a certain level, perhaps we know this is where we came from, and this is where we will return eventually. Human separation from infinity is only temporary, after all. To know this gives me comfort sometimes. At other times it makes me lonely beyond belief.

A day contains an infinity of space, and a day, in its old diurnal way, also contains an infinity of time. A day has its own movement and its own measured pace, minute by minute, hour by hour, whatever frantic counterpoint my thinking may try to beat against it. A day is just a day, and then there will be a night, and then another day. Life has been exactly like this since time began, every day with an ebb and flow like the tides, or like my own breathing, in and out, out and in, every minute, every second, right here, right now.

When my sister was in the hospital for the last time, six years ago, we talked about the comfort of "right here, right now," the breathable quality of the phrase—"right here" (breathe in), "right now" (breathe out)—and the way it kept immediacy within reach, and infinity at bay. Anne was not much interested in infinity, or in abstractions, either. A writer of fiction and fantasy for children, she once told me that she thought reality was overrated, and she showed no patience during her illness for any of the death-and-dying philosophies or scenarios then in vogue. She played with, or sometimes decorated, whatever unpleasant realities were truly unavoidable, so that when her hair was shaved off on one side of her head for an operation, she kept it long on the other and always wore a dangling, gaudy earring on the short side and a small, gleaming button earring on the long. The dispenser of prophylactic gloves on the wall in her hospital room might be used for the production of puppets or balloons; in the chemotherapy ward, she giggled with the nurses and played poker with her visitors. Three days before she died, at home, when she had eaten nothing for days and was gaunt and full of tubes, someone came into the room where her family was gathered to offer the visitors tea.

"Where's my cup?" my sister asked brightly, and she got one.

When we breathed together in the hospital, right here, right now, Anne and I were borrowing from Buddhist meditation practice, but we both would have been quick to say that we were not Buddhists in any bona fide way. In our family we were raised to be familiar with the spiritual writings and traditions of many religions, but we felt embarrassment about officially attaching ourselves to any religious practice, as if to do so would be pretentious. It may be that for my famous parents during our childhood years, joining a church, like joining a country club, would have risked unwanted attention and publicity. Better to have the Lindbergh children home-churched, as so many children are now homeschooled. Still, I don't know why we grew up so spiritually self-deprecating. ("Yes, I meditate, sort of, but just privately, at home. Of course it's not the real thing . . .") Buddhists or not, all of the women in the family have done Lamaze breathing for childbirth and a few of us for dental work—"Are you hyperventilating?" one worried hygienist asked me, picking away at a tenacious clump of tartar—so why not breathe for infinity, too?

The only thing is, I don't know whether Anne ever really did it. Maybe it was just me. I try to reclaim my sister from her death and keep her with me by using the first-person plural when I write or think about her: "We believed," "We always said," "We told each other." But I wonder whether it is a true unit, this "we," or whether I invoke it retrospectively in the possessive nostalgia of grief. Was Anne actually participating in the breathe-in-breathe-out "right here, right now" exercise I offered her, or was she, more likely, just glad to have my company and to hear the sound of my voice? When I think back to that time, I can hear the sound of my words but not hers, except for once. When she was hospitalized suddenly in Portland, Maine (a different, earlier hospital), for brain surgery, I heard the news and drove there as soon as possible to see her.

"I knew you'd turn up," she said to me sleepily, smiling from under a turban of bandages. I remember that, and her way of saying it, and how welcome it made me feel. Yes, I turned up. That's what I do. That is my family job. I turn up, often bearing flowers, but always bringing myself, and words. Words are the family legacy and the family habit, and they are what I have to offer, whether anybody pays attention to them or not. If somebody doesn't want to listen, he or she can go to sleep. I don't mind. I'm just doing my job.

Anne was enigmatic, anyway. Even if I could ask her, "Did

you like my words? Were you with me, right there and right then? Were we thinking and breathing together?" she might just smile at me again, with affection and mischief mixed in her expression, and say, "Maybe."

Now, in the echoing silence of her absence, and in the different silence of our mother's old age, I look again for words, not for my mother or my sister but for myself. I search for words as if for traveling companions on a journey I did not expect to be taking alone, and I look first in the family collections.

I read Anne's poems, most of them unpublished during her lifetime, and I find one written after a time when we were together. When I read it, I shiver, as if she had left it on purpose for me to find today.

(*A Visit from Reeve*)

A walk in the field
opened too many windows.
A narrow escape.
Turn your back to the wind,
Bustle home to fold sheets,
butter bread.
And when you wave goodbye
Laugh—say "soon"—
My sister, myself.

My father, too, has messages for me, and they often connect well with my own thoughts. In the last paragraph of my father's posthumously published book, *Autobiography of Values* (New York, Harcourt Brace, 1978), I find reference to the infinite again, in my father's sense of his place in the universe, and perhaps in the implication that he felt his own approaching death as well:

> *I grow aware of various forms of man and of myself. I am form and I am formless, I am life and I am matter, mortal and immortal. I am one and many—myself and humanity in flux. I extend a multiple of ways in experience in space. I am myself now, lying on my back in jungle grass, passing through the ether between satellites and stars. My aging body transmits an ageless life stream. Molecular and atomic replacement change life's composition. Molecules take part in structure and in training, countless trillions of them. After my death, the molecules of my being will return to the earth and sky. They came from the stars. I am of the stars. . . .*

Looking at this page, I am also amused, with the old, childishly irreverent amusement that is familiar to me from years of living with my father. In another paragraph I find a characteristic example of what was, in my hypercritical view at that time, his peculiar use of certain words: "The farther we penetrate the unknown," he writes, "the vaster and more marvelous it becomes." I suddenly remember how often my father used the word "penetrate," a common aviation/aerospace term, in his writings about rockets and missiles. They would "penetrate the unknown," or "penetrate through stars," or achieve some other "penetration." How this favored word in his vocabulary, especially in this context, made me giggle behind his back! I can see myself, in the late 1960s, with my miniskirts and my fishnet stockings and my paperback copies of the works of Sigmund Freud. Penetration, of all things, Father! How phallic of you! How male! How completely unconscious!

Finally, I find another page to ponder today, but very differently, in my mother's unpublished notes. These were written a year or more after my father's death, and I am reading through them this autumn, for possible publication. My brother came upon this material unexpectedly in a file in the Connecticut house. Her thoughts here are completely new to me, and her words very fresh. I am both fascinated and moved as I read. Here are her own immediate impressions about being alone and aging, notes that she made in the raw time of early widowhood, and which she had intended to edit later for a book she used to refer to as a *"Gift from the Sea* for Old Age." She was not able to complete this book, due to the complications of her own old age, but I am hoping to find, and pull together, enough material to do it for her.

The page I am reading now was written just after she had been to the Abbey of Regina Laudis, in November 1975, twenty-four years ago next month. She was an occasional and familiar visitor to that community, and an experience there that November inspired her, like my father in his autobiography, to write about death and the stars. But it was his death, not hers, that preoccupied her, and the stars were those by which she had flown with him years earlier when they were both in their twenties and charting air routes all over the world together after he introduced her to celestial navigation.

I went to the Monastery for Vespers, supper, and a Passion Play the Sisters were performing afterwards. Between supper and the play I went outside, already dark, and walked up and down looking at the sky. The stars were out, the patterns somewhat obscured by hazy patches here and there. I was confused and saddened that I could not find the familiar ones. Cassiopeia's chair I could pick out, and that must be the North Star. But where is the Dipper? And Orion's Belt? And the navigating stars? Can that be Castor and Pollux? Have I forgotten so quickly? If C. were here he would point them out to me. "Remember," he would say, "that isosceles triangle points to Capella. Then follow around, Capella—Castor—Pollux—Procyon—"

But after the play ("The Dream of the Rood"—to Mahler's 1ˢᵗ symphony—very moving, the tears were silently down my cheeks) I went outside again, on my way to the car and home. Looking up I saw all the stars blazing in the sky above me, suddenly clear, familiar, unmistakable, blazing out their confirmation.

There they all were, just as they always had been, unmistakable as a familiar voice or a well-loved face. There is Orion's Belt. There are the flock of Geese (Aldebaran). There is the isosceles triangle pointing to Capella. And there the circle of navigating stars follow around: Capella, Castor, Pollux, Procyon, Sirius. So dazzling was the spread of constellations that it had the impact of a vision, of some hidden insight. I drove home saying to myself: The dead, too, are like this, blazing within us—invisibly.

I walked home from her house the other night, with the stars out, and I could not recognize any of them. I was told so many times, by both parents, how to find the Navigator's Circle, and I loved the litany of navigating names used by the early pilots ("Capella, Castor, Pollux, Procyon, Sirius . . .") and used before them by many other names and in many languages, by the seafarers—Magellan, Columbus, Cortés, and all the horned and hairy Vikings in the children's picture books: Leif the Lucky, Erik the Red. I keep forgetting this knowledge, probably because I don't need it the way the Vikings and my parents did. But I also try to forgive myself my own forgetfulness, because if it is true that I don't always know the names of the stars, it is also true that the stars don't know them, either.

Walking down from my mother's house on a starry night this November, I was more preoccupied by the evening we had just spent together than by the heavens. She had commanded again: "Take me home!" This time I told her the truth, that I didn't understand her. Usually when she talks this way, I try to offer answers ("It's too late to go anywhere," "But you *are* home, Mother"), but this time I thought I'd try a question, the one that always rises in me at such moments: "What do you mean?"

"I mean my home!" She was firm, loud. What did I think she meant, for heaven's sake! How dumb could I get?

Still, I persisted. "But you've had so many homes, and this is one of them. I can't quite understand you, Mother, even though I keep trying. Sometimes when you say 'home,' I wonder if it's a real place or more like a feeling. Do you know? Is it a place, or is it a feeling?"

She paused, considered, then answered, "It's a feeling."

Aha! A little clarity, perhaps. Except that if my last words had been "Is it Connecticut?" she might have said "It's Connecticut." Sometimes she makes an affirmative statement out of the most recent question asked her, whatever it is: "Do you want to go to bed?" "I want to go to bed." "Are you hungry?" "I'm hungry." So I can't be entirely sure that I know any more than I did earlier.

"Won't you help me?" She leaned over toward me as I sat next to her, and placed her hand—so pale!—on my arm.

"I don't know . . . I don't understand this very well." I was hedging, and she knew it.

"Won't you *try*?"

I smiled, tried to think of something to say, but I paused too long to satisfy her urgency.

"You're not helping!" she scolded.

I laughed. I couldn't help it, and the mood of the moment changed.

We read together for a while from *The Illuminated Rumi,* a gift to me from my older stepson, Eli Tripp, last Christmas. I like Rumi because his poems can be simultaneously insane and wise, making absolute sense and at the same time no sense at all. He is well suited to us, to my mother and me, just now. We read poems about insanity and about sacredness, poems about wings and poems about water, about drunkenness, about fire. In the middle of one page there was a painting of a small, bright bonfire, and my mother pointed at it.

"I feel like that," she said to me.

It was insane, it made sense. I nodded.

"Yes, it seems like that. Something burning in you, something consuming," I said to her.

She held my arm and stroked it as I read, and after a while, very slowly, she seemed to tip over toward me. I thought she might be falling asleep, so I looked around to see if she needed help—a pillow, a caregiver's assistance on the way to her bed. But that was not it, not at all, because then I felt her lips on the hair of my arm, and on my skin. She was kissing my arm, over and over, and she was murmuring, "I think you can help me . . ."

What? What could this be? What was happening? I went numb. She lifted her head, she looked so white and so weary. The words weren't right, and I fought against them: too dependent and pleading, too dramatic, not like her, not for me. I looked at her face, taking in every detail, shocked by what I saw. There was a tiny shred of something orange—carrot paring or orange pulp—at the corner of her mouth, and a bubble of saliva right next to it. Oh God, not this. This isn't right. Let this stop now, whatever it is.

I touched her face, smoothed her hair, patted her cheek slowly, kissed her, smelled the dry smoothness of her forehead. These things are always the same. This softness, this smell of familiar skin against my face, this never changes. This stays without saying anything and goes straight to the heart.

The living, too, blaze within us, Mother, visibly, invisibly, you within me.

3

November 1999

The bee who goes
To the aster knows
December's fear;

The butterfly
On a daisy's eye,
That death is near;

Flies in the sun,
That summer's done;

Ripe berries wait
Their certain fate.

In red and gold
The lesson's told;

In ecstasy
The end foresee.

—Anne Morrow Lindbergh,
   from "A Final Cry,"
   The Unicorn and Other Poems

The hamster died. It was one of a pair Ben got at the school fair, three years ago this October. He called them Squirrel and Nutkin, after the Beatrix Potter character Squirrel Nutkin, in the children's book of that name. I guess it was Nutkin who died, because Ben says so, although I couldn't really tell them apart and I'm not completely convinced that he could, either. They lived not exactly together but in twin terrariums, side by side on Ben's bureau. Although they came to us as siblings, two Chinese dwarf hamsters curled up sweetly in one tiny compatible ball, after a few months they fought bloody battles and had to be separated. After their last fight, I found myself dabbing Neosporin ointment with a toothpick on one of their torn infinitesimal ears, and thinking that if pain is to be respected when it is enormous, then it also must be respected when it is very small.

I found the dead hamster when I went to wake Ben up in the morning. It didn't look so bad to me. It was a little, furry death, just an unobtrusive leaning into the side of the terrarium, by the corner where the water bottle hangs. Stiff, of course, as I discovered when I put my hand in to verify the animal's condition. But there was nothing violent here, and nothing ugly: no seeping liquids and no grotesque positioning of limbs.

I thought immediately of the death of my sister's dog, Sydney, only a few weeks earlier. He was a terrier who had outlived his mistress by six years and was almost twenty, in dog years a Methuselah. Still he persistently lived on, year after year, doing well until this fall, when his back legs stopped working properly. At first he trembled when he moved, and then when he was quiet, too. Later he could only hop, as if the legs had been fused together in the back, though his terrier tail nonetheless wagged as furiously as ever when he dragged himself along. He confused us with his happiness.

Anne's daughter, Connie, and I took him to be put to sleep, both of us patting his head and cuddling him on the veterinarian's steel table, having wrapped him warmly in an old black-and-red-checked blanket. The needle went in and the dog, blessedly, did go to sleep, while one tear ran down Connie's cheek.

"I'm just remembering when we got him as a puppy, Aunt Reeve," she explained, as if embarrassed, while we continued patting, soothing, and murmuring. Sydney breathed evenly several times under our hands, and there was a hush in the room that was like snow in the air. Then he stopped trembling for the first time in many weeks, and then he just stopped. He was the same dog, in the same blanket, and we were still patting him in the same way, and it felt exactly the same except that he had stopped, and it was absolutely silent where he lay.

The unexpected quiet after the expected death came as a relief to me. It was very much like what happens in my mind when the snowfall, silent and inevitable, finally covers the ground and changes the season beyond doubt. Yes. Now you know. Autumn is indeed over. Winter has begun.

When I catch myself thinking these thoughts, as I did when I was standing over the hamster cage, I am shocked. What am I trying to do, anyway? Establish some kind of cozy relationship with death? The hamster's death, the dog's death, my mother's death in anticipation, my own death in rehearsal? How can anyone realistically expect to prepare for any death at all?

I know that my father tried to prepare, dying according to his own wishes (and thanks to the elaborate arrangements and accommodations of other people) on his beloved island of Maui, rather than in a New York hospital. He did his best to plan ahead consciously and meticulously: buying just the right plot several years earlier in the old Hawaiian churchyard in Kipahulu, then telling us about it in glowing descriptions I thought odd, like language in a travel brochure for eternity: "It's a beautiful spot, not far from the ocean, and in one corner, there's a lovely old tree. . . ."

The last summer, when he had been sick for many months and the doctors had finally told him there was nothing further they could do, my father left the hospital in New York and arranged to be flown to Maui, accompanied by his wife and his three sons, who came from all over the world to be part of this journey. Anne and I, with our young children, were together in Maine. During his final ten days in Maui, he consulted with the gravedigger, requested that certain simple hymns be sung at his funeral, and asked that specific items be placed with him in his coffin: a Hawaiian tapa cloth, a Hudson's Bay blanket. In death as in life, he planned to travel light, always ready for the local climate.

My father was buried in a grave eight feet square and twelve feet deep, according to Hawaiian tradition, with layer after layer of lava rocks around and above him. The farm boy from Minnesota who had flown the Atlantic Ocean was tucked inside a cliff overlooking the Pacific; the flier who had loved the land he flew over as much as the wings that carried him was suspended in the earth forever, halfway between sea and sky.

My mother planned ahead in her own way. She mused speculatively as we drove past the little graveyards of New England during the years between her husband's death and her own debilitation. Her concerns, characteristically, were more often aesthetic than practical. In her seventies, both conscious and conscientious, she began to look for a place where it might be *pleasant* to be buried.

"That's a nice one, don't you think?" she would say to me, pointing to a maple-shaded country cemetery at the outskirts of some Vermont or New Hampshire village, where the mossy headstones leaned sociably toward one another in the grass, and a crumbling stone wall bordered the road. She went back and forth on the issue of cremation, and on the scattering of her ashes. Should she have some of herself scattered over her husband's grave in Maui? It seemed only fitting, after forty-five years together, that she should be represented in his final resting place, but she certainly didn't want to dig up all those rocks and have herself sunk down inside the grave with him, in another heavy coffin. It might disturb his peace.

Besides, it seems to me that my mother has always had a lighter, more delicate spirit than my father did, though it was never any less strong. (It may have been stronger.) I suspect that her soul might need to be closer to the surface of things than his, to achieve its ultimate flight. Despite his long career in aviation, my father was happiest when well grounded. My mother is different. I don't like to think of her spirit struggling under the weight of stones.

My mother is a New Englander, by birth and by upbringing, and I think she always felt that Hawaii was too rich for her Puritan blood—an almost immorally warm and flourishing environment, fostering the riotous gargantuan bloom of flowering plants that, if they grew at all in the Northeast, did so only in brief abbreviations of themselves during the summer season, or in pots indoors as miniatures, or in hothouses, destined to shiver in an ice-glazed northern window, naked in their bright foliage and their exotic names: anthurium, bougainvillea, bird of paradise, and so on. But if she were cremated, she could then make several compromises and have herself distributed here and there: a little in Hawaii with my father; a little in Switzerland, where she summered happily for thirty years; perhaps a little in the familiar, bracing, salty waters of Penobscot Bay in Maine, or in the coastal marshes and inlets of Connecticut, haunts of the waterbirds to whom she offered feed for fifty years. Now she could offer herself entirely to the sea, unless she decided instead to be planted with the fall bulbs, dug in like so much commercial bonemeal, to benefit their blooming in the spring.

For my son Jonny's death, there was no possibility of preparation, except that the severity of his encephalitis at five months was itself a kind of death. It was the end of the healthy babyhood he had seemed to be having, and the beginning of the process of illness that made his actual death, not much more than a year and a half later, an echo. "He died twice," a close friend said to me, and I think she was right. But the first death was not a rehearsal, and its repetition did not provide any kind of comfort, none at all.

With my sister we had some warning, in the way that we did with my father. Anne knew about the statistics, and she was told quite frankly what her chances of survival might be. She was brave and direct. She boldly wrote in the living will she signed early in her final illness that she hoped her family would "have the guts" to remove life-support systems when and if the time came.

But it isn't guts you need when someone you love is dying, it's clarity. Courage is easy for a bystander. Perspective is very hard and becomes much more difficult with time. It is clarity, most of all, that is so often missing at the critical moment.

And what *is* the critical moment? How do you recognize that "the time has come"? What time is that? And who decides? Then there is the question of what is appropriate—or even bearable—for a family member to do, or refrain from doing, in order to fulfill the wishes of a dying person. The vital, thinking individual who signs a living will soon after diagnosis, when the prospect of death is unreal and inconceivable and far away, is not the same person who begs for painkillers, or gasps for water, or shouts in delirium, or lies silent with parched mouth opening and shutting inexplicably over and over at the end. What is "help" at this point? What has meaning?

"Help me!" my mother whispers to me hoarsely on these autumn evenings. How? I want to ask her. How? How? How? I don't know who you are anymore. I don't know who I am, either. I don't know what will happen from one day to the next. How can I help you?

Still, I walk up the hill and I sit with her every day, usually in the evening, unless I just can't make myself do it because of something that happened the last time. In that case I take a day off, stay home and feel guilty, and go back the next day. But most days I go up the hill, and we sit together for an hour or two. It's the only thing I can think to do for her, and for me, too, at this time.

The day after we read the Rumi poems, I went back to her house and copied out by hand two poems that I liked and remembered from the night before. I wanted to take them home to think about. My mother was reading when I came in, but she stopped and looked over to watch me writing down the poems, line after line. I knew she was watching, so when I was finished, I showed her the piece of paper I'd copied the poems on. She took some time to read them both, nodded, and put the paper on the table in front of her before going back to her own book. I looked to see what it was.

That evening she was reading from *Living Buddha, Living Christ* by Thich Nhat Hanh. She seemed to be studying it, the way she studies books of prayers, reading each one over and over. In a moment she handed me the open book with her finger pointing to a paragraph on the right-hand page.

"Read this," she said. I took the book and read the paragraph while she waited. It was a passage about meditation. It explained the place of meditation in daily living, in the clear, poetic language for which the author is noted. When I finished reading, I handed the book back to my mother with an appreciative comment. ("Yes," or "That's fascinating," or "Thank you for showing me.")

She did not resume reading. She began, unexpectedly, to talk.

"Do you believe it?" she asked me.

"Yes, I think I probably do," I answered, reflecting upon what I had just read.

"I believe it," she responded, "but I don't practice it."

"I don't know about that," I said, protesting, expressing something I think could be true, both about my mother and about meditation in general. "I think maybe you do, Mother. Silence is a practice . . . Reading is a kind of practice . . ."

"Do you practice it?"

"No, I don't think so . . . well, maybe a little, but not exactly." A few feeble thoughts slipping out. I want to be truthful, but these days I am more uncertain than anything else.

We both sat silently for a while, then she spoke again, too softly for me to hear.

"Excuse me?" I asked.

"I think you live it," she said to me.

I was flooded with gratitude and discomfort at the same time. It was so good to know that she had thoughts about me!

But, like the kissing of my hand the other day, these particular thoughts seemed to be taking the shape of flattery, and flattery does nothing for me. I almost never believe it. Most of all, I don't believe it from my mother at this time in our relationship, when I can't tell, on any given day, whether she is offering me false coin or true.

"I don't know," I said again, thinking that this at least was honest. I don't know much. Too often I don't know anything.

We had dinner together, then afterward we sat longer, until my mother seemed to notice for the first time the piece of paper with the Rumi poems on her table. She picked it up and folded it perfectly in half, then folded it again, each time as carefully as if her ultimate intention was to create something beautiful and intricate, like a paper snowflake or an origami crane. After the smallest fold, when the paper could be folded no more, she opened it up again completely and began to tear it apart slowly along the folded lines.

I watched, amazed, as she tore my paper quietly, painstakingly, into many, many small and equal pieces. More than fifty, I thought, then realized it would have to be a multiple of four because of the way she folded the paper in half, then half again, and then again. Maybe sixty-four pieces altogether. A pile of confetti in her lap, which she covered up with her blue flowered cloth napkin and then hid from sight, like a little picnic lunch in a little bandanna in her lap, both hands folded over it, nothing left to be seen by prying eyes. She darted a glance at me, evasive and defiant. Who was I now for her? I had no idea. Who was she for me?

Next she unpinned and took off her brooch, a mother-of-pearl circle I'd brought her once from Florida. She tucked it inside her turtleneck tunic, close to her skin. I watched her without comment, trying to maintain a mild and friendly expression, trying to breathe evenly and quietly, but there was an extra pulse beating very fast inside me somewhere. Oh, where are you now, Thich Nhat Hanh? And what am I supposed to do? Breathe in and be a mountain? Breathe out and be a flower? I can still breathe, or at least I think I can, but I have completely forgotten how to be.

Then my mother turned from me as suddenly and completely as if I had scolded her. All of her movements became furtive, her body curled away and averted, her mouth moving repetitively but without sound. I tried to hear something, then I tried to read her lips, in case she was actually trying to communicate. I don't think she was, but after watching for a while I was pretty sure that if there had been a noise to accompany the mouth movement, it would have been a rhythmic hum, something like this: "Mum-mum mum-mum mum-mum mum-mum."

That was all I could figure out. I was watching very closely. I am always watching very closely, even though, so far, I haven't learned much.

All the same, there is something that keeps me hopeful when I am sitting with my mother. I don't feel hopeful when I am away from her. Going through the days of my own life this fall, I feel in limbo, at best. I am often sad. I am frequently anxious, or depressed, or impatient. I am periodically numb. But when I am actually with her, sitting beside her and watching, or reading, or sharing a meal, or just breathing along in her company, then there is a kind of hope.

What could it be? What is there to hope for? I can't explain the feeling, but I think it may come from simple intimacy. It is good just to sit next to my mother, whom I have known and loved for so long. It is good to know that her small body still fills a familiar amount of space in the room and in the world. In some profound way, I am reassured by her physical presence, sieved though it may be with a multitude of her absences: absence of mind, absence of spirit, absence of relationship, pending absence of life. Because of all these absences, when I am away from her I don't want to go back again. But because of that intimacy of presence, when I am with her I don't want to leave.

"Partir, c'est mourir un peu" ("To leave is to die a little") is a French phrase that my mother used to repeat, and it conjures up in my mind anguished European lovers, parting from each other in black-and-white movies with subtitles and trench coats, steam trains and railway platforms and lovely languid white arms waving from windows for the last time. Whenever he heard this phrase, my French brother-in-law always used to grin and add, *"Et mourir, c'est partir tout a fait . . ."* ("And to die is to leave completely").

Dyings and partings now begin to reflect and represent one another, so that when I walk down the hill at night to my own home, my son doing his homework, my husband watching television, and the puppy sleeping on the couch next to him, I always wonder to myself in the darkness of the night, which is so mysterious and infinite, so vast and so universal, so embracing of life and death and stars and cold air: "Is this the last evening?"

But it never is. There is always another morning, and my mother awakens into it, and I wonder whether she meets herself again, bewildered, every day. Does she sleep in peace in the old identity and wake into confusion in the new? Sometimes when she wakes up, she is angry. Sometimes she is sad, or completely foggy and disoriented, or in pain. At other times she is quite happy and may lie in bed for a long time and talk or sing to herself, the way I remember my own babies doing in the mornings before anyone else was up. On a musical day, she may conduct music from her chair in the living room, with both her arms waving in some real rhythm, guiding an imaginary orchestra. And there are days when she smiles as she moves, bending more and more this year over the walker, her face almost parallel to the floor as she makes her way slowly, slowly, across the room.

Lately it has been hard for her to get up at all, and once when I went in to see her in bed, late in the morning, she looked terrible. I thought that she must certainly be near death. She couldn't possibly make it through another day. Her face was socket-eyed, her flesh seemed dried up and her skin too close to her skeleton, as if the liquid had drained completely from the area and there was no space left anymore between flesh and bone. There was a white, fish-belly puffiness in her cheeks. Her eyes were half open, staring, but I had the feeling that she couldn't see. She seemed to have no sensation, to be just barely breathing. How could she sustain a day's life, or an hour's, in such a condition? Yet she did get up that day, and she did have her breakfast, and she did get dressed with the help of her caregivers as usual, and she did, many times, move across the room. By late afternoon, when I visited again, my mother was drinking tea.

"Would you like sugar?" she asked me.

A few days later, we asked a man who is a hospice nurse with the local home health care agency to come and visit her, once a week. The caregivers think that it is time for her to have more frequent medical monitoring beyond the regular doctor visits. They think that she is now beginning the real business of dying.

"How do you know?" I asked Ann Cason, leader of the care team.

"Too much is happening," she said to me. "I think maybe six months, if nothing else occurs, like an aneurism, or something of that nature."

"Six months?"

I looked at Ann, she looked at me, and we chuckled. Ann Cason's care team, indeed her whole care system, is widely known as "Circles of Care." Ann has professional caregiving experience going back for several decades, in both the United States and Canada. Her work is based in part on Buddhist principles and further informed by her own research, experience, and expertise.

All the same, we chuckled. So many times in the last six or seven years, one of us has been sure that my mother was in "the last year of her life," or "would probably not be here next year," or "was on her way," but it has never been true. Last year Ann, all her experience notwithstanding, said, "I'm not making any more predictions!" and I agreed. I even came up with a new way of thinking about my mother's condition, and shared it with Ann and my brothers, hoping it would help us. Our mother has been close to death for years, I said, but it is perhaps a kind of *geographical* closeness, not necessarily a closeness in time. She is on a border, treading close to the line, but there is no way of telling when she will decide to, or happen to, go over. In the meantime, we cannot make predictions. We cannot make plans. We must instead live a border life and make concessions to both sides—a little life here, a little death there. Check the will and take inventory of significant possessions so we know what is there and what she wanted done. Don't, of course, make any distributions, because these things are still hers. Think about a funeral service, look for the notes she left on this subject—what venue? what readings? what hymns?—but don't actually plan anything, because she is still alive. Better to plan the routines for life: plan a menu, plan a party, plan a visit from an old friend. (Plan it soon—but don't make predictions.)

We make predictions anyway. Six months, says Ann . . . by Christmas, I thought yesterday . . . before I come at the end of January, said my brother Land this morning. Is it just "wishful thinking" as Land himself suggested the other night? We want this long dying to be over, we feel it almost is over, we feel that it is time for it to be over, and then . . . it is not over, again, and again, and again. This is very frustrating.

Does my mother know? Does she feel that people around her, people who love her, are yearning for her death? Does she know that we think she may be yearning for it, too? I don't know. I'm not sure that what I really yearn for is my mother's death, anyway, but I definitely want the end of her frustration, and my own. I want this, knowing that when the frustration ends, I will not necessarily feel satisfaction or release, not for more than a brief time. I know that what is in store for me after the frustration ends is grief, and that grief, too, is long and anything but simple. I know grief well, and I dread it, but I look forward to it, too. It will be, at least, a change.

The nurse, Arthur, who examined my mother the other day for the first time, has a kindly, unobtrusive presence and a thorough manner, as well as a trim reddish beard. She liked him, I could tell. She often opened her hand in his direction, as if wanting him to hold it, and finally he did for a moment. I sat across the room during his examination, watching while he asked my mother questions to which she responded by nodding or by shaking her head.

Did she feel any pain?

"No" shake.

Did she mind if he took her pulse?

"No" shake, more assertive.

Could he examine her feet for swelling or blisters?

"Yes" nod, very emphatic, up and down and up and down and up and down.

As Arthur was leaving, I waved to my mother from across the room and blew her a kiss. She wiped her mouth, then waved back, one-handed. Then she lifted the other hand and waved with it, too. First they were back-and-forth waves, like Queen Elizabeth from her limousine window. Then they were little individual finger-waves, in rippling movements, reminding me of finger plays I used to teach the children in my nursery school years ago: individual digits waving, then a few together, then one after another in a rapid sequence like playing scales on the piano.

I copied her movements with my own hands, being her mirror. Then I made my arms move a bit more, conducting the invisible orchestra at a slow tempo, and she began to copy me. I made bigger and bigger movements, with deep breaths to accompany them. She made bigger and bigger movements, too—weaker, more fluttery, droopy-winged.

"This is great for breathing, Mother!" I exclaimed once. (Why, oh why, do I always have to talk?)

We continued in this way for some time, until I let my hands down to rest in my lap, and she did the same. A dance of hands across the space of her room, and then the dance was over.

Everything was completely quiet when I left my mother's house to walk back to my own home that day, and there was a feeling of snow in the air.

4

December 1999–January 2000

I try to remember the horizon on the sea. Perhaps it seems a simple thing to remember, but I never can create again in my mind that boundless-what-is-beyond-the edge feeling.

—Anne Morrow, class of 1924, from
  "Distance Lends Enchantment," *The Wheel*,
  Miss Chapin's School, March 1924

We have six inches of snow, Christmas has come and gone, and my mother is still very much alive. It is now the middle of January and the weather has been cold. Sometimes, at night, the thermometer falls as low as twenty-five below zero. My mother sleeps and eats and sits in her chair. Sometimes she talks, sometimes not. I am not sure reading means as much to her now as it did two months ago. There are times when she reads, but just as often she simply looks across the room at the fire. I have the feeling that if there were no fire there, and no fireplace, she would still look in exactly that same direction and in exactly that same way, like a woman looking through a window, or out to sea, intent on some fixed horizon.

Over the past few weeks she has become interested in the closer view, too, and busies herself with the things on the table in front of her, accessible to her fingers. She arranges and rearranges the stones and shells and little animals for long periods, seeming completely absorbed by this task.

Before the holidays were fully upon us, I kept this in mind. I went shopping for a finger-smooth Christmas gift for her. I wanted something that she could touch, and touch again, like her stones and shells, or like her stuffed robin, or like the flat, velvety pillow with bright yellow and black stripes, colored like a bumblebee but shaped like a fish, which was a gift from Sue Gilman, one of her caregivers.

Sue is from Atlanta, Georgia. Like each of the caregivers on the team, she has found her own ways to relate to my mother, through a combination of intuition, practice, and trial and error. One night in December, when my mother seemed particularly agitated and miserable but uncommunicative, Sue gathered all the Rilke poetry she could find in the house, and read out loud with my mother until well after midnight. Poem after poem, each one rich with insight and veiled in romantic obscurity, they spoke aloud together, into the winter night.

"I figured we'd just get right to the bottom of this sucker," Sue said to me later. "I wanted to get to the heart of it." This approach seemed to work, or maybe they just tired themselves out. In any case, eventually, my mother slept.

You never know what will work, just as you never know what will be important to her from one day to the next. The velvet fish-pillow has become recently essential. The caregivers call it her "Bumblefish." They pick it up and offer it to her from time to time, at transitional moments; just before

dinner, for instance, when everybody else is busy with prepa-
rations and my mother is sitting alone looking at the fire.

"Here's your Bumblefish, Mrs. Lindbergh. Would you
like it?"

She puts out her hand, and when she receives the fish, she
holds it against her chest and caresses it, holding it close like
a kitten, patting it gently from dorsal fin to rounded black and
white belly, over and over and over and over. The rhythm is
sure, the movement endless.

I wanted to give her something like that, something soft
and smooth, something she would touch again and again with
her fingers. Every time she touches my soft, smooth finger-
thing, I thought to myself as I looked in the stores before
Christmas, she will be touching me, in a way, whether she
knows it or not. I liked this idea, and I imagined several possi-
bilities: another stuffed animal? A miniature box of polished
wood? A necklace of translucent beads?

Finally, at the cashier's counter at our local bookstore, I
found a basket of what looked like rounded stones, actually
small globules of clear glass about an inch in diameter, a little
like the pieces of sea-worn glass Anne and I used to find together, walking along the beaches in Maine.

The stones at the bookstore were man-made and of uniform size and shape, though they came in a variety of colors:
indigo blue, bottle green, purple, or clear like droplets of so-
lidified water. Each one had a word etched in it in the kind of
lettering I associate with very old Vermont gravestones, or
contemporary books bearing titles like "Celtic Wisdom."

"Surrender," I read on one of the stones, "Acceptance" on
another. In the context of my mother's long dying, the words
made me thoughtful, and as I picked up these first two stones,
I was strongly tempted by them. Maybe I could offer her, in

this way, a gentle subliminal message to help with the ending of her life, something that would be felt through the whorls of her caressing fingers, then seep into her unconscious: Surrender, Acceptance, time to let go . . .

No, I decided, I could not. What kind of Christmas gift would that be from a daughter to her mother? It was like giving her a shove, a nudge in the ribs, to edge her closer to the precipice where a hint, a breath, a puff of wind could send her over.

"Acceptance, Mother." (*Get it?*) "Surrender . . ." (*If you know what I mean.*)

I don't think so. Not for Christmas.

I moved on to other stones with other words on them, and finally chose seven nondeadly sentiments: "Bravery," "Courage," "Grace," "Harmony," "Intuition," "Tolerance," "Trust." These, I thought, would offer my mother inspiration for life as she knew it now, rather than for death. It seemed a kinder impulse during the holiday season.

Meanwhile, my son Ben stood near me, intrigued. Then he, too, began picking up the stones he thought were most interesting. "Money," he found, then "Power," then "Persistence." No grace and harmony for him! No surrender, no acceptance, no death in his lexicon.

However much I may be thinking about her death these days, I doubt that my mother thinks about it at all, any more than Ben does. She does not talk about dying the way she used to six years ago, after we lost Anne. She did not talk about Anne's death then, only her own. She would pace the floor for hours on end, saying "I am dying, call the doctor." She left notes all over the house—"I am dying . . ."—and signed her name at the bottom: "Anne Morrow Lindbergh."

I found several of these later on fragments of shopping lists, notepads, the backs of torn envelopes. One, especially, touched me—"I am dying, but peacefully . . . tell my children . . . Anne Morrow Lindbergh." I did not believe it—not that she was dying, not that she was peaceful, but I kept the envelope. It reminded me that at least she knew she had children.

When Anne was dying, there were moments when our mother seemed to understand what was happening. Once, during that last week, we wept together, and she embraced me and offered words of comfort: "You never did anything wrong, Reeve." The words were so sweet to me, coming from her at such a moment. I wrote them down in my diary, and later I included them in the book I was writing about the family.

I did not write down what she said to me on the day of Anne's death, however. It had taken a while to gather the courage to tell her that Anne had actually died. When I finally managed to get the words out, she looked me up and down, then said with what appeared to be fastidious disdain, "Is *that* what you're going to wear to the funeral?"

Today such a response from her would seem ordinary, if inappropriate. Then her words were like a knife in my heart. I couldn't repeat them to anyone, couldn't admit I had even heard them. At that time, I still believed that every word she uttered must be some version of the truth.

Now I think my mother often just says whatever comes into her head. Her words may be triggered by anything in her immediate environment. Was I very casually dressed, the day Anne died? Maybe wearing jeans and a sweater? Was my hair messy? Did I look haggard from lack of sleep? Or was it herself she was thinking about? Was she still wearing a nightgown when I told her about Anne's death? Did she look down and see a flannel sleeve with rosebuds and a lacy edge at the wrist?

I am sure she knew something terrible had happened to

somebody, and that something formal was required of somebody else. The rest may have been beyond her, or else she, like me, was shocked and stunned by words.

She exists in a state of great fluidity of being, as if in some watery suspension like a womb of consciousness, where all notions and conditions are interchangeable: identity and propriety, fashion and manners, day and night, life and death.

She does not, however, talk about death, dying, or doctors anymore. She does periodically talk about getting married. A year ago, she said that what she would most like to do in the New Year was to marry again. This year, just before Christmas, the same theme recurred. My brother Jon and his wife were here, decorating a small fir tree we had brought into Mother's living room. They strung little white lights and hung her Scandinavian wooden ornaments, from other years and other homes, along the branches as she pointed to the places where she thought the decorations should go. My mother watched Jon and his wife for a while quietly, then she asked Jon if he loved her. He told her that he did. She asked him next if he would marry her. A caregiver explained to her gently that he was her son, and already married. As far as I know, she did not ask him again. But she has spoken to her other two sons in the same way, and has more than once assumed that one of them was her husband, just as she often assumes that I am her sister or her mother. When the time of confusion passes, our individual family identities may reassert themselves, or they may dissolve entirely.

"Do I have to do my homework now?" she asked me one night last week, as we sat together eating dinner. "No," I said, "you don't have any homework tonight." "Good," she said. That was all she needed to hear from me, whoever I was.

Instead of homework, I gave my mother a little story that

my daughter had sent me from graduate school by e-mail. It goes like this:

> The English professor asked his students to punctuate a sentence.
>
> All the men punctuated it one way, all the women another.
>
> *Sentence: A woman without her man is nothing*
>
> *Men's punctuation: A woman, without her man, is nothing.*
>
> *Women's punctuation: A woman: without her, man is nothing.*

I read this out loud, amused, then handed it to my mother. She studied it at length without cracking a smile.

"What do you think?" I prompted. "Which one do you like best?"

She has not spoken to me at all, not in words, for a week or two. Instead, she points, or nods, or shakes her head. Without hesitation, and unmistakably, she lifted a deliberate finger and slowly picked out the "men's" punctuation. A woman, without her man, is nothing.

Damn. That wasn't the response I wanted. I was foolishly disappointed and couldn't let go of the feeling. Knowing it made no sense, I wanted to confront her, to scold her, to herd her back in the direction of her former self. I wanted to shake her by her tiny bowed shoulders, wake her up to who she was.

You know that's nonsense, Mother! A woman without her man is lonely, yes, I know that's true, because you told me so. Of course you were lonely, surely you must have been angry, too, weren't you? I would have been! Your husband must have seemed so free, he who could continue to travel on and on, through the world you had discovered together, on wings, when you were explorers and lovers and partners . . . then later, when the children came, you were the one who had to stay at home to raise them, in anguish at first—grieving for the first one, left alone with all the ones who came after. Who wouldn't be lonely? Who wouldn't be angry? How did you manage? So much of the time, all by yourself! And you did. You did it all. You were really something!

So where do you get this *nothing*? "A woman, without her man, is nothing"? Baloney, Mother! How could that be your real opinion? You were without your man for much of your marriage, and yes, you were lonely, but you crafted from that loneliness a way of life: independent, thoughtful, creative. You made a gift of that loneliness and offered it to millions of women. You wrote *Gift from the Sea*, Mother. You can't mean this: "A woman, without her man, is nothing." What's the matter with you? Stop it!

Stop it. Don't abandon your principles. Don't be uncharacteristic of yourself. Don't be strange. Don't be weak. Don't forget who you are. Don't surrender, don't accept, oh, don't die, don't die, don't die, after all. Forgive me, I didn't mean it . . . don't die, Mother!

"Who exactly *is* Anne Morrow Lindbergh?" Ben asked me when he came home from school, looking at the cover of one of my mother's books, which was lying on our kitchen table.

"Your grandmother!" I answered, surprised. I was surprised in the same way when one of my daughters asked, years ago, "What *is* the Berlin Wall?" I am always astonished that these names, these powerful elements in my own history and the history of my time, have so little meaning for my children.

"Well, I knew it was either her or Ansy," Ben quickly said in his own defense, sensing my reaction.

"Ansy was Anne *Spencer* Lindbergh," I explained neutrally. Ben nodded, and wandered off.

He is tolerant of, but not yet deeply interested in, his grandparents' famous history. When I travel and am asked to talk about my family, I often tell the story of visiting the Air and Space Museum in Washington, D.C., with Ben for the first time, in 1997. He was ten years old, and this was his first glimpse of his grandfather's airplane, the *Spirit of St. Louis*. We were allowed to enter the museum early, before it opened to the public, and were invited to climb into the bucket of a cherry picker used for the maintenance and cleaning of the aircraft, which is suspended from the high ceilings. Up we went, higher and higher, Ben and me and the operator of this machine, until we were right next to the *Spirit*. I was able to reach out and touch it for the very first time in my life.

I put my hand on the handle of the cockpit door, realizing that my father must have done this hundreds of times when he was twenty-five years old. So young, and yet so long ago, seventy years before his grandson's visit to Washington. I thought of my two daughters, now in their twenties. My older daughter, Lizzy, was herself twenty-five that year. She is the only one of my children who knew her grandfather at all, and she was two and a half when he died.

I had tears in my eyes as I turned to my son, standing next to me there in the bucket of the cherry picker, high in the air of the Air and Space Museum in Washington, D.C., so close to the *Spirit of St. Louis*, whose young pilot was a grandfather he would never know.

"Oh, Ben," I said, almost whispering, "isn't this amazing?"

"Yeah!" he responded enthusiastically, full of delight. "I've never been in a cherry picker before!"

And to this day, I think that of all the things Ben might have said at that moment, nothing could have pleased his grandfather more.

I envy Ben his ease with our family history. It has been so hard for my own generation to come to terms with the "Lindbergh" in our lives. I find that when I try to make cohesive sense of the personal and the public past, to make the two fit together, it doesn't always work. We five, the first generation, grew up with our parents as familiar family members in our home, not public figures out in the world. I knew Charles Lindbergh intimately for twenty-eight years of my life, and yet there are many things about him that I am not familiar with at all. I can remember how my father walked, and laughed, and opened a door, and combed his hair, and ate his breakfast, but if someone asks me for specific information from before the time I knew him, the famous time, I have to look it up.

Although my father died in 1974, before many of his grandchildren were born, I worry about each generation of our family as it comes of age and confronts his history. The Lindbergh name means different things to different people. Reactions can be extreme and contradictory. There is still hero worship in some quarters. People who focus on the 1927 flight from New York to Paris might meet a member of my family and say, "Lindbergh! He was the greatest American hero of all time." But those who are most concerned with my father's political activity before World War II might say, "Lindbergh! He was no hero! He was pro-Nazi, wasn't he?" or "He was anti-Semitic." There is frank curiosity, often "You're a Lindbergh? How does it feel? What was it like?" Sometimes there is simple compassion: "Lindbergh . . . that kidnapping . . . my God, how awful. You people have had so much tragedy. How do you survive?"

I have always found this last reaction touching and, for

some reason, surprising. I am glad to know there is still sympathy for my family, among all the other responses. And yet I always want to say, "How does anybody survive?"

I have a long list, a kind of internal litany, of thoughts about the family history, especially as it relates to my father. I think that he became famous not only because of his 1927 flight but also because he represented then, and continued to represent throughout his life, much of what America was in the twentieth century. I think that the combination of adventure and exploration and technology was an intoxicating mix for my father, with his Swedish pioneer ancestry and his love of machines.

I think that the kidnapping death of my brother in 1932 came at a time when media sensationalism was at its height, and that sensationalism was deeply entangled in the event, from start to finish.

I know that my father, a leading isolationist before World War II, did not ever consider himself pro-Nazi or anti-Semitic. I don't believe that he was ever pro-Nazi, I never knew him as anti-Semitic (he certainly did not raise his children with any such beliefs), and I trust that he was unconscious of what I consider the implied anti-Semitism of some of his written words from the prewar period, just as he was unconscious of what I think are the racist implications of others.

Here, again, he inescapably represented aspects of his generation and of his era, as I inescapably represent mine, as my children will represent theirs, and on and on. If people look back over their family history, isn't it likely that they will find political and social attitudes that are embarrassing and run counter to today's? And are we really better people than our ancestors were because we have the perspective of time? What will our descendants think about us, I wonder.

It strikes me this season that my mother must be free of her own fame now, just as she is free of the details of memory and the burden of personal relationship, the burden of personal response. Some things from the past linger for her here and there: a wisp of memory, a shadowy dream of loss. For a few days this winter, she asked her caregivers anxiously about a child she believed to be in her house. Could they see him? Was he all right? Was he hungry?

When I heard about this, I thought sadly that she must be referring to her own lost baby, dead since 1932, my brother Charles. There was no way to know if this was true, and no reason to trouble her mind further with questions. The moment passed, and the child, again, was gone.

"I think we see only a tiny fraction of what's going on with her," my brother Land said today in a telephone conversation. "Most of the process is deep inside somewhere. That's where everything is happening."

I had told him that I thought nothing at all was happening, that she was in a kind of stasis, not suffering or anxious, not anything in particular. She was just eating, and sleeping, and passing the time quietly. Changes in her health and strength were almost imperceptible. I could see none unless I looked back over the months and realized that she was not quite as active, not quite as verbal, not quite as present in her body.

It is not frightening or unpleasant for me to be with her this month because she has been so apparently content. She is not angry, she does not accuse me of hating her, she does not express that yearning to go home. For the most part, my evenings with her are comfortable. The greatest challenge for me in my visits is the change in pace.

At my own home, I am busy all the time. I may be writing at the kitchen table, or working at the computer in my office, or making telephone calls, or doing kitchen or laundry tasks. But all day long, whatever I am doing, I tend to be in motion. I am a reluctant and distractible writer, with poor self-discipline, so that even when I am working, I move a lot. I get up and go downstairs and get a glass of water, I wander through the rooms looking for a book, I let the dogs in and out through the kitchen door. If I'm really restless, I go out to feed the chickens in the barn, or I get in the car and drive into town, shopping and running errands and taking Ben to school and going to the post office.

But at the end of the day, when I go up to visit my mother, I walk through the door of her house and all movement stops. Nobody, here, is going anywhere. I sit down, I drink tea, I read, I talk to the caregivers, I watch the fire. I absorb the quiet, and for a while I go quietly crazy.

Nothing happens, I think. Nothing will ever happen. She will live forever, and her life will always be exactly like this, quiet and slow, so very slow, minutely detailed, focusing on meals, and the bathroom, and the tiny things on her table, pills and stones and Rilke's poetry, and the black and yellow Bumblefish.

Last night the fish was a bit sticky in places, with what looked like dried egg yolk. Sue Gilman gave a little grimace when my mother picked it up, not long after I sat down beside her. "We really need to give him a bath," Sue said.

After a while, I begin to sink into the environment, and I begin to like it. After a while, I don't want to go home. I don't want to be in the house where all that motion takes place. I want to stay here, in the house where nothing happens and nothing changes.

Thinking this way last night, I remembered suddenly that

Mother has not spoken to me for many days, and that it has seemed to me she does not have the energy to make conversation, even a conversation of one or two words. I remembered, too, that she has not been out of the house at all for weeks, since a visit to the doctor before the holidays. The weather is very cold, she hasn't had much energy, and she has expressed no desire to go out. The caregivers are trying to keep her moving around indoors as much as she can tolerate, since her sedentary life has begun to affect her body. Her feet are sometimes swollen, and lately she has had one or two red places, the beginnings of pressure sores, from sleeping for many hours at a time in one position.

Once or twice during my visits, my mother will get up from her chair and move toward the bathroom or bedroom, laboriously making her way out of the chair and across the room with the help of a walker and a caregiver at her elbow. Then she comes back again and sits.

I watch the process and help where I can. It takes a visible effort for my mother to get up and move, even this little bit. But as I watch her, I am amazed at how much strength I can see in the effort. Even though she is in the weakest condition I have ever witnessed, I am conscious, more than anything else, of her strength.

While I was with her last night, the nurse, Arthur, came in to examine my mother's feet. He carefully took off her shoes and her socks, one by one, and set them aside. Then he placed her feet together, heel to heel and toe to toe, on a hand towel that someone brought for him from the bathroom. He picked up one bare foot at a time and examined it, in a thorough and unhurried way, indeed so slowly and carefully that the whole process looked to me like a slow-motion sequence from an old film. He gently touched the red places, rubbed on lotion and massaged her toes, and put a foam bandage on a small pressure sore on her ankle.

"Does that feel better?"

She nodded, looking at him, her face impassive.

He wanted to check her lungs with a stethoscope, slipping the metal piece inside the back of her sweater and listening. She had been coughing slightly all day, and when he brought the stethoscope out, he reported that there seemed to be a little liquid in the lower left lobe of one lung. She had had pneumonia in the left lung back in June, so we discussed whether she should visit the doctor again or just increase her doses of Lasix, which reduces water retention and which was prescribed on an "as needed" basis. Arthur and I and Ann Cason talked quietly together about this, including my mother in the conversation by directing questions and suggestions to her, whether she responded to them or not. She did not.

Arthur thought it might be a good idea to check for fever.

"May I take your temperature, Mrs. Lindbergh? This is a digital thermometer, it can go right under your arm. Is that okay?"

"Yes." Her voice was hoarse, but she gave him a real word along with the nod. She likes Arthur.

There was no fever. We decided to try the Lasix, but to call the doctor if she still was congested in a day or two. Arthur left to drive home for the evening, and Ann Cason and I sat and talked together for a little longer, while Sue Gilman started preparing dinner.

My mother did not speak or move, and she did not pick up a book or touch the stones and shells in front of her. Soon I had to go home to my own house for the night. I leaned over and kissed her forehead, and as I stood up again, I saw that her feet were together in the same position where Arthur had left them, heel to heel and toe to toe. She had her shoes and socks back on again, with her shoelaces neatly tied.

When I left her that evening, she was holding her Bumble-fish cradled in her arms, very close to her body, and she was looking straight ahead, into the heart of the fire.

5

March 2000

Then only, when man's inner world is one
With barren earth and branches bared to bone,
Then only can the heart begin to know
The seeds of hope asleep beneath the snow;
Then only can the chastened spirit tap
The hidden faith still pulsing in the sap.

Only with winter-patience can we bring
The deep-desired, long-awaited spring.

—Anne Morrow Lindbergh,
   from "No Harvest Ripening,"
   The Unicorn and Other Poems

In a Vermont spring, everything seems to thaw, melt, dissolve, and get soggy all at once. Nothing feels solid. After a frustrating between-season period of weeks, when snow and freezing rain alternate, the winter collapses into wetness. The snow gives way to rain, the ground to mud, the maple trees drip with sap for syrup, and the mood both indoors and out softens in anticipation of something new, something better, just about to happen.

At my mother's house, there is little change, just a deeper and more consistent silence. My mother has not died, and as far as I can tell, she is not dying. But she is slower, even slower, though I did not think it was possible she could slow down any more.

I think of her as the perfect example of a conundrum I heard long ago in school and have puzzled over ever since, as I have puzzled over the notion that if somebody lifts a calf every day, someday that person will be able to lift a cow. (Is that just a joke, or is it true? Has anybody ever tried it?)

Here it is:

If a person takes a step toward a door, and then takes another step half the size of the first one, and then a third step half the size of the second, and then a fourth step half the size of the third, and so on, will that person ever actually get to the door?

I suppose the answer depends on how far the person was from the door to begin with. You could bump right into it on the first step if it were a step away. But let's say it's across the room. Then what? This is the way I think about my mother's movement, whether toward her bathroom or toward her death. It happens so slowly that I don't believe it is happening at all.

When she sits in her chair all day long, as she usually does unless she stays in bed, every few hours someone comes over to her chair and suggests to my mother that it might be a good time to get up and walk. Then she rises, with support, and takes the handles of her walker, and prepares to move. As I see it, every part of this sequence takes tremendous effort on her part. At every stage, the whole process is in doubt.

Will she get all the way up onto her feet, or will she sink down again in her chair? When she is up finally, can she stand on her two feet for long enough to steady herself? When she is steady, will she have enough energy left after the exertion of rising and standing to take one step forward? If she takes one step, does she have the strength to take another?

The whole thing seems inconceivable, yet I watch it happen. On the inside of my mother's frail body, where it counts, the heart and the will are as strong and firm as the arms and legs are weak and unsteady. And so, as she has always done, she prevails.

She is up. Long pause. She is steady. Longer pause. She is moving, at her infinitesimal pace.

Watching her move across the room, helper at her elbow, is like watching the tide go out on the long, rocky beaches of North Haven, Maine, where my mother and I both spent our childhood summers. I can tell there is movement, but only in relation to the things that mark it: a clump of seaweed, a boulder, a relic lobster buoy, bleached and barnacled, each object in turn measuring the position of the receding waves.

Now in her own tidal progress, my mother passes the arm of her chair. Now she is at the edge of the rug. Now the wheels of the walker sound on the hardwood floor, and she is in navigable waters, clear sailing, slow and stately rolling, all the way to the bathroom.

Time continues to feel suspended in my mother's house, but the circle is drawing in. Many circles are drawing in: the circle of movement, the circle of pace, the circle, I believe, of interest. She sits and stares, uncomplaining, unless someone offers her an alternative: "Here's a book you might like, Mrs. Lindbergh"; "Here is a letter that came for you, Mother"; "Here is your dinner"; "Here are your evening pills"; "Here is a fresh cup of tea."

I think she accepts what is offered out of ingrained politeness but would be perfectly content to sit and stare and do nothing else. The rest of us are not content with this, however. It makes us uncomfortable. We want her to be doing something, thinking something, reading something, participating in some way that we can understand. So we give her books to read, food to eat, flowers to arrange ("Where should the roses go, Mrs. Lindbergh? Here? What a good idea. Should the stems be shorter? Yes?"), or laundry to fold ("Why don't you do the washcloths, Mother?"). She participates in the daily round of household activities when invited, but I think she does so only as a courtesy for us—not for herself.

I sat next to her last night, reading, and she, too, had a book in her hands, one that had been offered to her. ("Here are some books that might interest you, Mrs. Lindbergh. Which one would you like?") She chose the one closest to her, naturally. She was very well brought up.

She appeared absorbed by her own book as I read mine and the caregivers went about their work: preparing dinner, washing sheets, feeding the dog. It was a peaceful time for us all, everyone deep in her own task or occupation. But I sat for an hour by my mother's side and finished the book I was reading, and while I was reading, I looked over and noticed that during all that time with me, she was holding her own book in the appropriate position for reading, as I was, and running her eyes appropriately across the lines, as I did, but she never once turned a page.

The circle is drawing in. Curiously, I do not interpret this as loss, but as intimacy. I look at her more closely, more intimately, and more gently. I let my eyes rest on the contours of folded skin in her face and take in, like an inhalation of sweet fragrance, the softened, faded, sunken quality of the folds. She seems to me like a wilted rose: fair and pink and petal-soft, surrendering, still scented.

I linger over each awareness of her. I see that the skin of her hand is pale ivory, fragile in texture as the silk of an old wedding dress. I see that her fingernails have been neatly trimmed and polished by Janet White, the cheerfully soft-spoken stylist who comes to the house to do my mother's hair and manicure each week, and who is married to our postman. I like to watch Janet working with my mother, who is now so completely, so uncharacteristically, willing to be touched. Her head is cradled while her hair is brushed, her hands are held as her nails are trimmed and professionally polished and then lotion is rubbed into her palms. My mother, who once so resisted physical tenderness that I wondered during childhood if it was an imposition to kiss her good night, now submits to care and coddling as never before. Her previous body-shyness has melted away, as she is touched over and over by careful, caring hands all day long. Hands lift and lower her into and out of her bed, hands clothe and feed her, hands clean her: teeth, hair, fingernails, breasts and belly, private parts. She has finally let herself go now, giving herself up with no comment at all, falling lightly as feathers and silently as snow into our waiting hands.

My mother's own hands are clasped together in her lap now. They are the hands of a well-behaved child of her generation, with shiny shell-like ovals at the ends of pale fingers beached in stillness.

"The sacred hands," says Laurie Crosby, observing my gaze, smiling at me and at my mother. Laurie is not a Buddhist. She has a New England Quaker background, and grew up with her sisters on Cape Cod. Tall, slim, and supple of body ("willowy" is the word that comes to mind), Laurie has a deeply intuitive spirit. Right now she knows what I'm thinking. She has some of the same feelings and thoughts. I look again at my mother's hands and suddenly wonder if they are deliberately placed together in a position of prayer. Is her silence a prayer?

The house is so quiet that my attention wanders away from her to objects around the room. I follow her gaze and I try, like my mother, to stare, just to see what that feels like. I watch a candle on one end of the mantel over the fireplace burning more slowly than its counterpart on the opposite side. I look for a long time at the rocks I gave her at Christmas, and notice that they have been joined in their stone dish by two little stone Easter eggs, someone else's holiday gift for spring. I observe the three beanbag birds on her table: the robin, a blue jay, and a duck, side by side, beaks lined up and beady eyes staring back at me. The Bumblefish has disappeared, and instead there are, interchangeably, two new stuffed animals: a green tortoise about the size of a hot-water bottle and a smaller, bright red and black ladybug, both gifts from Land. She holds them one at a time flat against her chest and strokes them in rhythm, as she did the Bumblefish, top to bottom.

When Arthur comes, twice a week now, he checks the blister on her ankle. We are still keeping it bandaged because it does not change. It does not heal, and it does not get any worse. It stays the same.

She looks well; her complexion is pale but not gray or sickly in the least. She has color in her cheeks, her eyes are the same clear blue. Her gaze is direct, but I don't know what she's looking at. (What are you looking at, Mother? What do you see?) She needs to be reminded to eat, or even given the first few bites of each meal to get her started, though she eats well once she gets going.

She is always elegantly dressed, usually in a pantsuit, or slacks and a sweater of pink or pale blue or lavender. She wears a patterned silk scarf around her neck in a matching color, carefully arranged by a caregiver. My mother does not object when silk scarves are arranged around her neck by the kindly hands of strangers, who then step back to look, smiling and tilting their heads.

She looks lovely. Hands, hair, fingernails, sweaters, and scarves. She has become a flower arrangement, an ikebana. She does not mind. Or if she does, she doesn't mention it.

The last time Land came to visit us, for three days, he told me that the whole time he was here, he heard her speak "no more than two dozen words." I envied him. Twenty-four words! I am with her every day, and some days she does not say even one word to me. If I sit patiently for an hour or so, though, I may hear her speak to the caregivers, or to the room at large. Sometimes the caregivers will tell me things she has said while I wasn't there, which gives me the feeling that the minute I leave the house, she gets chatty.

"We asked your mother if she liked her dinner," Laurie laughingly reported to me one night, referring to the fact that my mother's food now has to be cut up small or pureed, because she has trouble swallowing large pieces. "And she said, 'Well, maybe if I knew what it was.' She keeps us all on our toes, in her humorous way."

She does?

On a different afternoon my mother was reading to herself from a book I had brought her, a new anthology of poems and prayers for children. I worked on this book for several years, gathering and editing selections that were sent to me, or that I had ferreted out from my reading, and they came from all over the world. There are Hebrew prayers and Celtic poems, African canticles and wise sayings attributed to saints and popes and scholars, an excerpt from Anne Frank's diary and a Richard Wilbur translation of a poem by Francis Jammes about donkeys and God. This had been one of my favorite projects.

The first bound copy had just arrived in the mail, and I brought it up that same day for my mother. I have always given her the first copy of each book published, since she has been my mentor and my inspiration all my life and, in years past, my most appreciative reader.

As soon as I showed the book to her, she became completely absorbed by it, which was a great satisfaction to me. At the same time I found myself secretly fretting, worried that she would get my book all sticky. My mother will read while she eats, if she can, and the food and the books inevitably mingle, though the caregivers try hard to keep the two separate.

If I want to read one of her books while I sit next to her, I often have to pry the pages apart. When I do, I find dabs of dried jelly or egg yolk stuck between them.

"May I take your book, Mrs. Lindbergh? We can put it aside right here," said Catherine Clark when she brought over a tray with tea and a snack. Catherine Clark usually can persuade my mother to do what is reasonable. Catherine has always reminded me of Greta Garbo. She has deep brown eyes, a low voice, and a wave of auburn hair that frames her face in a manner reminiscent of Depression-era film stars. Catherine put down the tray and reached out her hand for the book, indicating with her other hand a small table next to the chair.

Some days my mother relinquishes her reading material to the caregiver; other times she hugs a book to herself tightly and will not let it go.

This time she did not let go, but she did say yes in her raspy whisper, and I heard the word, though I had to lean forward to catch it. A moment later, still holding the book, she looked toward the window and observed, in the same rough voice, "No stars."

I followed her gaze, trying to understand. Yesterday was the first sunny day after a week of rain. Now it was about three o'clock in the afternoon. The sky was blue, the clouds high and scattered. Bright sun, no rain, no stars.

"No stars in the book, maybe?" Catherine suggested, casting an eye at the window and then at the anthology in my mother's lap. I knew Catherine was still standing in front of my mother because she intended to remove the book in order to preserve it. I wondered if she'd get away with it. My mother looked at Catherine and said nothing. Relinquished nothing. A standoff.

I didn't say anything either, because whenever I try to converse with my mother these days, she neither talks to me nor acknowledges that I am talking. It's as if I'm not there. I don't even exist.

I take this much too seriously. I start thinking very fast, and the thinking is childish and irrational: she does not talk to me anymore because she no longer loves me. I know it isn't exactly true or is irrelevant—she doesn't need to love, she needs to *be* loved just now—but the thought speeds into my mind, and before I can protest, it turns into another one: she is not talking to me because I am not worth talking to. Then I think she does not talk to me because she doesn't love me and I'm not worth talking to and I have betrayed her—I don't know what that means, but I have suspected it ever since I began to take care of her, ten years ago. She did not want care, and my insistence seemed a betrayal.

The negative thinking hurtles on down from there. I can't help it. I think my mother doesn't talk to me for all the old slimy reasons I discovered when I was thirteen, the things about me that everybody knows but nobody will tell me: I smell bad and I am ugly and stupid.

That's it. Rock bottom. Time to go. I get up and kiss my mother on the forehead and walk home.

Ann Cason says that the silence of an old person drives us crazy because we all long to be "confirmed," and this silence, so common to the old with their diminished health and strength and declining interest in conversation, is the ultimate lack of confirmation. It is the most difficult aspect of caregiving, and the chief reason that caregivers "burn out" over time.

If I speak to my mother and she doesn't respond, at first I think there is something wrong with her in a medical sense (Is she deaf? Is she dead?). Quickly, however, I begin to believe there is something wrong with *me*. I can fight it, but I still feel it, and it doesn't go away.

To lose such an important listener in life is like losing my shadow. With no shadow, does a person truly exist under the sun? With no listener, does a person really have a voice? Silence means so many things to human beings. Some of them are unbearable.

A very odd thing happens when my mother's silence drives me crazy: for a while I stay crazy, even outside her house. Because she has no words for me, I start to question and generally distrust words. Because she has chosen silence, I fear that her silence may be superior to everybody else's noise. If she has chosen silence, why haven't I? Since I make my living with words, as my mother did before me, this kind of thinking puts me on shaky ground professionally. But often, these days, that's exactly where I am.

If I go out to speak to a school or organization, I'll suddenly panic in the middle of the speech, overcome with the fear that my words make no sense and that I'm babbling meaninglessly, blah blah blah. When that happens, I quickly pick up the paperback copy of my most recently published book, and I read short excerpts from it, gaining confidence from the printed page, or from the fact that the page is indeed printed. My words, printed. Therefore they must have meaning, for somebody. I think, "At least I *used* to know how to use words." When I feel better, I put down the book and go on talking.

In the same way, when I write a book review or a short piece for a magazine, I am repelled by my vocabulary. If I use the word "extraordinary" to describe a new author's talent, I look at it and frown. Extraordinary? What does that mean? "Exceeding the ordinary." What a tired, stupid, boring word. I try "insightful" instead. It looks facile and pretentious. I cross it out. "Intuitive"? A wispy word, fluting and foolish. I hate "intuitive," too. In fact, I'm sick of all the words I know. I'm sick of words, period. I wish I could be silent, like my mentor, like my mother.

At our house this spring, the old dog died and the lambs were born, one of them to a neglectful young ewe who fed him for the first day or two and then forgot about him, or more likely just abandoned him in favor of his stronger, more aggressive twin, not knowing any better. Nat found the baby ram unconscious in the sheep stall one morning and brought him into the kitchen alive and breathing faintly, but very cold and limp. We didn't have much hope as we rubbed him with towels and cursed the stupidity of the species, something we have done annually for twenty years. How could any animal survive through the centuries with so little intelligence? Who said that the only thing dumber than a sheep is a rock? And why were we still raising them, for that matter? Or trying to resuscitate a lamb that will just get eaten anyway? At this point we started to question our own intelligence and quieted down.

The lamb unexpectedly revived, and in the warmth of the kitchen, he stood up on wobbly legs and began to bleat frantically and incessantly for food. We gave him powdered milk replacer for lambs from the feed store, mixed with warm water, every four hours in a Miller Lite bottle with a heavy-duty black rubber lamb nipple fitted over its mouth. We did this for six weeks, except at night, when the lamb—unlike my own babies at the same age—slept soundly.

I love having a bottle lamb, in spite of all the feedings and the cleanup. Maybe because there is the immediate satisfaction of having that noise stop—infants are tyrannical, and whatever the cry is, human or ovine, the pleas for attention are devastating and cannot be ignored:

"*Hey!* I'm *starving* here! This is an *emergency!*"

When the breast or bottle arrives, the noise stops, and the satisfied rhythmic suck of survival begins. Once that happens, no matter how compromised the infant may seem, life is taking hold.

The funny thing is, I think what I have always loved most about this process is that it is wordless, and now I love it more than ever. When I am feeding the lamb, I just feed the lamb. I don't think about it. I get away from both my mother's silence and my own speech. I do the job at hand, and I'm happy.

6

June 2000

To ———
She pondered still the earth, each passing mood,
Each hour, long known to her was wondrous yet
Who counted all the shreds of loveliness;
The slippery gloss of lilac-leaves, rain-wet;
And, silken soft to touch, the inside coat
Of chestnut burs; velvet of rain-soaked bark;
Winged seeds of maple, twirling; and the still
Magnolia blossoms, moon-bright in the dark.
These things she pondered as a lover might
Finding all beauty tremulously caught
In some slight gesture, dear beyond belief:
A tilt of head; a brow puckered in thought;
  A way of pushing back a lock of hair
  Carelessly, so, to leave a temple bare.

—Anne Morrow,
  The Smith College Monthly, May 1927

Our wet spring has turned into summer in just a few weeks,
and suddenly the landscape, so reluctant to change for so

long, is in full bloom. Lilacs and wild roses scent the lawn and driveway, and wild iris grows in the swamp. The wood thrush sings in the woods by my mother's house at night, and the cliff swallows chitter and squeak under the eaves of my home in the morning. They nest here every year, two or three families at a time, building their homes, which looked to me alarmingly like hornets' nests, just below the roof and right next to our bedroom window, until I learned what they were.

Nat tells me that although barn swallows and tree swallows are plentiful here, cliff swallows are rare in northern Vermont. Ours is one of three known colonies in the area. There is another in some high, sandy cliffs overlooking the Connecticut River, and a third at the Agency of Natural Resources in Waterbury. Because seeing these birds is so unusual, a biology professor at a nearby university brings his classes here every year to observe their behavior.

I am not at all surprised that we have a colony of rare swallows on our roof. Nat's farm has always been a haven for creatures, from orphaned foxes to injured porcupines to the annual bottle lambs. Our little spring ram, though weaned now and out in the pasture with the other sheep, still runs across the field at full tilt, bleating, whenever he sees a human being.

Nat theorizes that certain animals simply discover over time that they are safe here, like the cliff swallows, who have learned through many nesting generations that we don't keep cats. Other animals come to us by chance, like the porcupine he found lying wounded high on the land once, or the baby fox brought to him years ago by an earlier dog. He treated the porcupine's wounds with disinfectant and offered it slices of quartered apple by hand to combat dehydration. Soon it was able to travel on. The fox, too, stayed with us only until we were able to contact a friend who was a wild animal veterinarian with a license to keep and treat foxes.

I think the animals keep turning up because of Nat himself, who has had wild creatures in his life ever since he was a small boy: crows and skunks and a flying squirrel named Alcibiades who came and went through his window in the New York suburb where he grew up. Now he's in his mid-fifties, and the word is out through all the natural kingdom. Here in the northeastern corner of Vermont, there are probably invisible signs posted all around his farm, like the code left by hoboes traveling through the country in the 1930s. "Trust this man," they say. "Good for a night's lodging, for first aid, for food, and for sanctuary."

Or it may be that Nat goes out looking for the animals, consciously or unconsciously. The first autumn I was here, he and I were driving to town over a back road with some friends when he abruptly stopped the car.

"Look," he said. "Over there." He was pointing at the crotch of a tall maple tree beside the road. I couldn't see anything at first, but then two small heads appeared, with pointed noses and dark rings around bright eyes, staring right at us. They were raccoons, unusually small ones, in plain view and in broad daylight.

"There's something wrong," Nat said, and got out of the car. He was standing about ten feet away from the tree, shading his eyes and looking up at the pair.

What happened next is something I would not believe if I hadn't seen it myself. The two baby raccoons climbed out of their hiding place and crawled very fast down the trunk of the tree, then ran over to my husband. They crawled up his pants, clawed their way up his shirt, and came to rest on his shoulders, one on each side.

I saw this, and so did the two other people in the car. None of us will ever forget it. Nat said that he had heard of raccoons doing such things if in trouble, but nothing like it had ever happened to him. He assumed these two had been orphaned and perhaps treed for a long time by whatever animal had killed the mother. They were weak and thin, no bigger than kittens. He got in the car on the passenger side, and I drove while he held the raccoons.

We took the pair home, and because they seemed undernourished and dehydrated, we kept them in a big chicken coop in the barn for a few days, offering them food and water. We released them after that, thinking they might stay around the farm for a while, recovering, but then they would take to the woods.

The trouble was, they wouldn't leave. For months, those two raccoons were in and out of the house and the barn, investigating everything in sight, eating the dog's food, destroying property, and demanding our attention. The dog seemed intimidated by them, and they were completely unafraid of humans. Quite the reverse, in fact. Although there was plenty of available food around the farm, they came running into the house lickety-split the minute the kitchen door was open, and they could tear open the trash and scatter it around the room in a matter of seconds. They loved to jump up into our arms and inspect our mouths for food, and tried to extract morsels of corn from my daughter's braces with their clammy little paws. It was impossible to leave the butter dish out on the table without having it grabbed and spread by these two bolts of furry lightning leaving greasy paw prints all over the house: on the sofa, the chairs, the beds, and our clothing.

The raccoons were impossible. We did not want them as pets, but they became pets anyway, the quintessential Pets from Hell. But we affectionately called them Bonnie and Clyde, and although we tried hard to keep them outdoors, we enjoyed their company in spite of their manners until the following spring, when they started killing chickens. At that point Nat collected them both and drove them to a wild area several miles away, by the river, and left them there with a week's supply of dog food and a sense of mixed relief and regret. He says he still dreams about them and continues to harbor the fantasy that they'll come back someday, with their children and grandchildren. I nod understandingly, smile at my husband, and pray they don't.

There are always new animals, anyway. In early June of this year the puppy, Elsa, now full-grown, brought home a live baby rabbit in her mouth. We had no idea where she got this animal, but feared it came from a plundered nest in the meadow. It appeared dazed but uninjured, except for a small bloody spot on its stomach. A wildlife-specialist friend to whom Nat described it thought this might have been an umbilical wound, since it healed quickly and was not infected at all. The rabbit itself was the size of a small chipmunk, covered with soft brown fur. Its eyes were open.

"Beautiful," breathed my husband.

Nat fed it evaporated milk hourly with an eyedropper, and went out every morning to collect the kinds of green things a young rabbit would normally eat. This is something he has done before with small wild mammals, and soon the baby rabbit, a female, was alert and thriving. For the past few weeks she has been riding around the farm in Nat's shirt pocket, where she appears content, drawing comfort from motion and warmth, perhaps, or just from being close to a beating heart.

She came up with him to my mother's house the first week,

and he took her out and cradled her in his cupped hand, offering the quiet little animal to my mother to touch. My
mother and the rabbit both drew back at first, then my mother
reached out one tentative finger and touched the smooth fur
between the rabbit's ears. Very lightly, she stroked it in one
direction, over and over, rhythmically, ritually, as if it were
a miniature version of one of her stuffed animals. The rabbit did not tremble or flinch at this, but sat perfectly still
until Nat gently withdrew his hand and replaced her in his
pocket.

Later in the week, encouraged by this scene, I decided to
bring my mother a box full of day-old chicks, two dozen baby
bantams we had ordered from Murray McMurray hatchery in
Nebraska. I brought them to her the very day they arrived in
the mail, and placed the cardboard box on her table un-
opened, so she could listen to the chicks peeping as she sat in
her chair.

She looked at it, then looked at me.

I held the box up so she could look through the round holes
in the sides of the cardboard and see all the tiny fuzzy bodies
moving around inside. "Baby chicks, Mother! Only a day old!
They just arrived."

She did not react at all, but I slowly started to lift up the lid
anyway. I wanted to show my mother all this teeming new life,
to expose her to the awakening of spring in this very tangible
way.

As I fumbled with the cardboard, she suddenly spoke to me
directly, for the first time in two months.

"Don't let them out!" she said sharply.

I looked up to see her expression of alarm. It occurred to me
that for this moment, at least, I was the unpredictable one,
not my mother. We had switched roles. Whatever other vi-

sions might be occupying her mind, one of them certainly was of me, right this minute, behaving irresponsibly with these birds. What did she think I would do? Spill all the baby chicks into her lap? Dump them out to run loose on the floor?

I was tempted, I really was. I imagined myself a poultry maniac. I could throw the whole box of chickens up in the air if I wanted, feathers flying and chicks peeping. I could scatter chicks like confetti, like chicken feed, strewing them all over the place. I could be the wacky old lady and my mother the one who watches and worries. Whoopee! What a possibility!

On the other hand, it might not be too good for the chicks, and my mother looked scared. I didn't want to scare my mother, not really. But it was fun thinking about it.

"I won't let them out. I promise," I said. And I didn't. I lifted the box lid gently, and we both looked at the baby chicks bobbing around, flapping their tiny wings, peeping and pecking, none of them much bigger than a Ping-Pong ball. Every one of them was fully hatched and fully formed, eager to be alive and one day old.

Here we are again, I thought. One more spring. Another batch of baby chicks, another growing season. How can it seem so much like all the others I've known, all the lilacs, all the lambs, all the baby chicks—and yet so absolutely fresh and new, the whole world revived and reinvented at the same time?

My mother herself has revived with the new season. She is not physically stronger, but she isn't any weaker, and lately she often seems more alert, more verbal. This is a bit of a surprise and, frankly, a bit of a shock to me. *Now* where are we going, I wonder.

I was so caught up in death and dying this past winter that it became a way of life. I really thought death was around us, that my mother's dying was in full swing. I knew it was happening very, very slowly, but I took it for granted that we were heading downhill, at least. The timing was uncertain, but the direction seemed absolutely sure.

I have given up on Ann Cason's six months, of course, and so has Ann, because more than seven months have passed since she made her prediction, and many weeks since she threw up her arms and abandoned it.

"All bets are off!" said Ann, and I have to agree with her.

Once my mother made it through the winter, we all knew she was going to be with us for a while longer. But as she became quieter and seemed more content, I made the mistake I always make. I started imagining again. I imagined that she and I would now have a slow, sweet, lingering good-bye. It would be gentle and lovely, and it might stretch out over the spring and the summer but certainly no longer. It was clear that I would have to adjust my thinking some. I would have to drop all those metaphors about "snow in the air" when thinking and writing about her, for instance, but maybe I could work in something about fading roses and falling petals. Things die every season, after all. There's always a good metaphor for mortality in nature.

But surely, I am saying nervously to myself now, as the lilacs go by and the peonies bloom and June turns into July, surely we're not going on further, into another fall and another winter, are we? Can it be that everything is going backward? That there's been a reversal, and my mother is getting younger, not older; better, not worse? Will she get stronger and stronger, rather than weaker and weaker? What do I do if that happens? What's going on?

We celebrated her ninety-fourth birthday on June 22, with cake and candles and neighbors and caregivers and friends, including my friend Catherine Thomas's mother, Rhoda, who is close to my mother's age and who arrived in a silk trouser suit, leaning on a silver-headed cane. Rhoda is small and elegant. She and her husband spent years in the diplomatic service in foreign cities all over the world. Rhoda's manners are impeccable, her heart is warm, and she has a great sense of humor, thank goodness. She sat on my mother's right side as the gifts were opened and the food was served. My mother took no notice of her presence, at least not at first.

From Sue Gilman, my mother received a bright orange stuffed fuzzy animal in the shape of a crab, which she held by its two front claws and swung back and forth as Arthur the nurse and I played duets in the background. Arthur plays the flute, and I used to play alto recorder and want to start playing again. We were using three small booklets entitled in German *Bachfreunde, Handelfreunde,* and *Mozartfreunde,* which we had borrowed from the neighbors, Laura and David Brody. The Brodys were at the party, too. They have a three-year-old daughter, Bea, who came from China, and the parents sing and play many different kinds of music on a number of instruments. They recently presented an informal concert at my mother's house with Arthur. David played his guitar and sang Newfoundland sea shanties. Laura sang a Hebrew lullaby. David and Arthur then played works for flute and cello, including a Bach piece especially chosen for my mother, because she has always been very fond of Bach.

For the birthday party, Arthur and I were less like concert performers than like strolling musicians at a Shakespeare festival, tootling away on the sidelines while the action takes place elsewhere. We played as the guests ate their cake and ice cream and admired my mother's gifts. Among other offerings, she had a few new and beautiful rocks for her collection, a recent translation of the Beatitudes with a red and gold cover ("Blessed are the meek," etc.), a huge spring bouquet with lilies and roses and delphinium, and several pairs of decorated socks: some with embroidered butterflies, others with angels, and one pair with the words "harmony" and "clarity." I gave her those.

My mother swung her crab by the claws, back and forth, forth and back, and then abruptly leaned over and pushed it against Rhoda's shoulder. Rhoda did not draw back, but patted the stuffed animal and smiled at my mother. "Yes, isn't that nice?"

My mother did not smile back. She just nudged Rhoda again, harder, with the crab. Watching this, I missed an F-sharp and had to drop out for a whole measure of *Bachfreunde.* Damn. *Play nicely, Mother. Please! Don't assault the guests . . .*

"Mrs. Lindbergh?"

Susan Shaw was watching, too, bless her heart. Susan Shaw was wearing a bright red dress. She is dark-haired and bright-eyed, with a vivid, cheerful personality and great presence of mind. My mother looked over at Susan and tossed the crab up in the air, over her table, over the heads of the guests. Susan gracefully caught it in midair.

"Oops!" said Susan, as in "Oops-a-daisy!" *Oh boy,* I thought to myself. Saved again.

It has been like this lately at my mother's house. Sometimes she will sleep for hours, maybe fifteen at a time, going to bed at nine in the evening and getting up in the middle of the next day. But when she is awake, often there is electricity in the atmosphere, and a feeling that anything can happen.

Once when I came in, she was maneuvering a trio of chocolate ladybugs around her dinner napkin, which was folded in an isosceles triangle. When I sat down, she placed a ladybug on each point of the triangle and looked at me.

My turn, obviously. I put a little stone in the very center, equidistant from each of the ladybugs. Behind the stone there was a whorled shell no bigger than a dime, but perfect. I picked it up and showed it to my mother. So small, so intricate, a "gift from the sea," a touch of magic.

"Lovely, isn't it, Mother?"

She looked at it, and then at a glass of grapefruit juice, half full, sitting next to a cut-glass bud vase at the edge of her table. The vase, too, was a work of art: a still life reflecting the glow and glitter of the evening lamp. It contained a single white lily.

She picked up the grapefruit juice. *Oh, no,* I thought. *She's going to throw it at me.*

She hasn't done this for about six years, but there was a period of tearing things up and throwing them, and for a few months, a lot of liquid went winging through the air. It was mostly water, only rarely something that would leave a stain, like V8 juice or red wine. And it was a long time ago. But were we spooling backward now? Could she be retracing the past ten years? Were we going to go through everything again?

But she did not throw the juice. She poured it carefully into the cut-glass vase and watched the water in the vase turn all milky. It looked as if some of the color had leaked down out of the lily, through the stem.

Next my mother picked up the tiny shell, the one I had admired, and daintily, holding it between her thumb and her forefinger, dropped it into the grapefruit juice, or what was left of it. Then she looked at me, and there was no doubt in my mind that the look was a challenge:

There, you little shell-worshiper. Now, go ahead. Make meaning out of that!

I burst out laughing. There was nothing else I could do. I laughed until there were tears in my eyes, and then I reached over and took my mother's head in my hand and kissed her loudly on the cheek.

She looked completely satisfied.

Another night this month, she asked me sharply, "How long have *you* been here?" when I had been with her for a couple of hours. At that moment she looked as if she had just woken up from a long, deep hibernation. She looked more awake than I had seen her for years, and I fell into another of my old snares, feeling a sudden jolt of irrational joy—*It's over! She's back! She's the way she used to be!*

I wanted to say, "Ten years. I've been here for ten years, waiting for you, Mother. Where have you been?" But her eyes clouded over, and I lost the feeling.

"I've been here since about six o'clock," I said accurately.

"It's really time for us to go now," she said with some firmness, as if I were eight years old again and dragging my feet at leaving a toy store. Enough was enough, her tone indicated.

"I don't know," I said, taken aback and faltering. "It's probably a good time for staying, Mother. It's late at night and you have your own nice bed here, and I have to go down the hill to Nat and Ben."

"Well, I can't stay here." She was adamant, rational. The store was about to close, and it was time to go home. That's all there was to it.

"Mmmm. It's pretty nice here . . ." I'd forgotten how this conversation was supposed to go. We had not had one like it since November. What was the next line?

"Couldn't I go to your house?" Oh, yes. That was her line. But what was mine?

"Mrs. Lindbergh? Here are your evening pills, in apple-sauce," said Karen Frazier, coming over to the table with a bowl and spoon. Karen Frazier is new on the caregiving team, having recently moved to Vermont from South Carolina with her three sons. In my imagination she is a motherly version of Marilyn Monroe, some years later in Marilyn's life. Karen has a cloud of silver-blond hair, moves softly around the house, and speaks in a caressing whisper. My mother's medications are too difficult for her to take now in pill form. She has trouble swallowing anything that is not pureed, including her meals. Mixing her pills in applesauce is a recent innovation. It has worked very well so far.

My mother turned away from me then and picked up her spoon, and settled into absence. I kissed her hair, whispered good night, and made my escape.

Another night, we did not talk at all, we just held hands while we listened to a CD of Andrés Segovia playing a Bach lute suite on guitar. Laurie Crosby and Catherine Clark were there. My mother and I were both drowsy, and she was again distant, hooded, unresponsive, but all the same, she was the one who took my hand as I sat there, rather than my taking hers, as usual. I didn't leave her house until about eight o'clock, and when I got up to go, Laurie, who had been reading in an armchair, said she suspected my mother and I had both fallen asleep at least once. She saw us, one in the chair and one on the sofa, with our eyes closed and our heads leaning toward each other, a mother-daughter tableau.

I wonder if we look alike.

7

July 2000

I thought that when one grew up nothing unpleasant would happen. Apparently nothing hurt "grown-ups." My mother didn't kick or scream in the dentist's chair, nor did she bite the doctor's fingers when he examined her sore throat. It was a blow to realize that when one grew up one had to be even braver though the pain was just as hard to bear as before— and did "grown-ups" really cry? It didn't seem possible but it was true. That was another proof that showed that things weren't pleasant when you grew up.

—Anne Morrow, class of 1924, "Disillusions of Childhood," *The Wheel*, Miss Chapin's School, March 1924

The next one to go was Ichabod the lizard. He died on a Monday, and I found him, because I always find them. Ichabod was very discreetly deceased, though. I wouldn't have known of his passing except that I have gotten into the habit this summer of going outside through the glass doors in the living room, right by his terrarium.

I go this way instead of the usual way—through the kitchen door and onto the front porch, then down the steps and the path to the driveway—because Nat has more or less remodeled the kitchen for the rabbit. She has tripled in size and energy since she came to us, and is in evident need of exercise.

We are not enthusiastic about releasing her into the wild right away. Because she came to us so young, she was instantly attached and dependent upon us for survival, and therefore will not rehabilitate easily. She licks Nat's face after feedings, sits on the dog's back, and jumps into my lap to nibble on my book as I read. For the time being, she is living in the house, and because of her size and energy requirements, my husband explained to me, we have to make certain adjustments.

The door from the kitchen to the porch is often closed, for instance, while the doorway from the kitchen to the living room has been fitted with a hinged, swinging, chicken-wire-and-plywood apparatus that Nat constructed. This looks like the door to a large chicken coop and can be fastened firmly with a hook and eye to the doorframe, allowing the rabbit to run freely around the kitchen.

For the rabbit, this arrangement is a chance to be free of the cage, but to humans—to this one, anyway—it feels a lot like being in one. Despite all my years of living in the country, I can't get used to washing dishes on the wrong side of chicken wire, so I spend much of my time in the living room and frequently use those doors to go outside.

I noticed the other day, as I was heading out to the car, that Ichabod had been lying a little too still for a little too long in the same place in his terrarium. It was the spot that he liked best, closest to the glass doors, where he would lie in the mornings on his log, and soak up the sunshine.

I reached in to touch him, but instead of darting away as my hand descended, he lay still and unresponsive, not a flicker. Uh-oh.

There was no doubt about it. He was stiff and rubbery to the touch, although he looked very handsome. He had died in his bright green phase, not the dull brown one. I found this interesting and wondered about it. Maybe it just happened that way because he was in the sun, something about chlorophyll, but maybe not. If I were a lizard and had a choice, I'd certainly want to die with my skin bright green, too. What point would there be in camouflage at such a moment? Why not go out in glory?

Ben and I buried the lizard in the garden, between a young rosebush and a group of bright orange daylilies, in full sun. Ben said, "Ichabod, you were a good lizard." He always likes to say a few words at these times. Under my breath, I gave a vague blessing along the same lines. I have discovered, after many years of experience, that I am incapable of grieving over reptiles. There is no relationship between us, and therefore nothing to mourn but their presence, which is minimal. But I always take them seriously, and I believe in treating them with respect.

We cleaned the terrarium out on the lawn, and as we tipped its contents onto the grass, dozens of crickets poured out of the gravelly bedding and into the sunshine, liberated from their fate as lizard food.

"I guess he didn't starve to death," said Ben. We had both worried about this. Had we neglected Ichabod? Did he have enough food and water? Was he sick? If he was, how would we have known? "They only live two to four years, you know," the man at the pet store told me when I stopped there later and told him the news. "And we never actually know how old they are when we get them."

The crickets scattered themselves over the wet grass, beyond our bare feet, out of their glass prison and toward the lush, enormous summer morning. Ben and I both watched, pleased to see them go. It was nice to balance one death with many escapes to freedom, everything vanishing together in green.

Summer in Vermont is so beautiful and so short that I always immerse myself in it, wallow in it, try to be as much a part of it as I can. I listen to the birds: the swallows in the early morning as I lie in bed, the thrushes at night as I walk up the road to my mother's and down again. The wood thrush on the hill above her house sings a pure, liquid song of just a few notes, so brief that it is over before I can be sure of what I'm hearing. Then it repeats, and I identify it and feel satisfied. The veery, far off in the deep woods, sings a different, longer song. It starts sweet and high, then descends with rippling fluidity, like a piccolo imitating a waterfall.

I watch for deer at the edges of the fields at dusk, while I'm taking laundry off the clothesline, and when I see them, the sight brings tears to my eyes. I don't know why. I garden in my perennial beds in the late afternoons with an eagerness that is close to gluttony. Digging and weeding and planting and tending my flowers, all this serves some primitive instinct, so that I feel much more like a pig rooting for truffles than a woman staking her delphiniums, or pulling up witchgrass, or transplanting phlox from a shady to a sunny spot. And yet there is a maternal quality to it, too. I spread cedar-bark mulch over the tender roots of young hosta with care and quiet delight, patting the ground with my fingers, tucking in my plants.

In the garden I love to feel every movement of my body, large or small. I love to smell every scent of earth and bark and sweat and leaf. The pleasure I take in my garden is so physical, and so intense, that I imagine it should be illicit or, at the very least, fattening.

I have come to identify with generations of women in their flower gardens, through the centuries, all over the world. I can only imagine what this intensive labor, this strenuous exercise in the service of nothing but beauty, must have meant to women in more restricted times. Here was a harvest beyond vegetables, a way of life beyond food and shelter and clothing and the drudgery of survival. Here was a life of color and shape and grace and smell and touch, growing right out of the dirt of the dooryard. Here was sensual delight!

I remember both my mother and my grandmother as gardeners, each with her own style. My grandmother Morrow, who lived at different times in Cuernavaca, Mexico; in Englewood, New Jersey; and in North Haven, Maine, was a woman of abundant means and generous spirit. She hired gardeners wherever she lived, and personally directed their activities with good taste and strong character. She brought garden notebooks with her each year from her winter home in New Jersey to the island where she summered in Penobscot Bay, and like the horticultural commander in chief that she was, she outlined her campaign plans for the distribution and deployment of battalions of flowers everywhere around her.

I can see the multicolored array of blooming plants in graduated sizes, on either side of the front walk between the white picket fence and the front door of her house in Maine, and I remember long perennial beds bordering the path to the rocky beach where we swam. If I close my eyes, I can see her snapdragons and her larkspur, her pinks and her foxgloves, and I think I can see her delphiniums. I can't see hollyhocks, and I doubt that they were there, much as I love them here at my home. There are more than half a dozen hollyhock stalks in full bloom now, outside my own front door, each growing higher than my head. The flowers are as big as teacups, blooming pink, white, yellow, and magenta. They look just right here. Hollyhocks are farm flowers, meant to gather around a door in Vermont like chickens. They are not flowers that an ambassador's widow would grow in her trimly edged flower beds. But surely my grandmother grew delphiniums, blue delphiniums, like mine. Isn't that why I love them and wait for them to bloom every summer? I think of them as my grandmother's flowers.

My mother, on the other hand, preferred trees or the most delicate of shrubs. I remember Japanese maple trees, forsythia in bloom, the blush pink of a flowering crab, or euonymus branches with their bare, intricately twisted limbs, a few of which she would clip regularly to put in a tall vase in her window. She had a few flower beds, including patches of pansies near the house, a cluster of lily of the valley at the edge of the lawn, and a strange little cactus garden on a rocky outcropping by the stone path. I think that must have been planted by the former owner. I can't see my mother as a deliberate cactus grower. It would be out of character.

She was not a flower gardener in profusion, the way her mother was, or the way I hope to be. But she could grow the things she wanted around her, and she could grow them by herself. I remember that far away from our house, across the driveway and up the hill only a few steps from her writing cabin, there was another garden, hidden away like a secret. That one was full of roses, with deep hearts and rich scents, and thorns so sharp they made me bleed dark red drops, like a princess in a fairy tale.

At my mother's house in Vermont, a garden project is under way this summer. Marco Alonso and Ruth Taylor are young artists in the area who hire themselves out as gardeners during this season. Marco has shoulder-length silver hair, pulled back and knotted behind his head with a disciplined yet decorative severity, like a samurai. Ruth is beautiful, with a gentler, rounder face, and honey-colored curls rippling out and down over her shoulders, giving her the look of the women or angels in Botticelli paintings.

Marco and Ruth have come to create perennial beds by my mother's back door. It is the first formal gardening effort since the house was built. They also intend to make the scrubby hillside bloom just behind her house. They dig up the beds by hand, enrich the soil with piles of "pond muck" that Nat brings up from the farm with his tractor and a bucket loader. Then they put in the flowers: lilies and calendulas and dahlias, lupine and rose campion and sunflowers. They come a couple of times a week, and when they finish working at the end of the day, they pick some of the flowers and bring them in to my mother to be put in bowls and vases.

When I visited last night, the house was full of flowers. My mother sat among them holding a well-dressed stuffed mouse between her thumb and forefinger. It was wearing a straw hat and a lacy dress, and it was about two inches high, a birthday gift from her oldest granddaughter, Kristina Lindbergh. Kristina, my brother Jon's daughter, was the first grandchild to call my mother "Grannymouse," the name by which she is known in that generation.

I admired the mouse, then sat down beside my mother to

read, as usual. It had been a busy day, and I was pleased to be with her at the end of it. I had spent much of the day corresponding with her admirers, specifically with aviation historians who are researching her accomplishments as a glider pilot in the early 1930s. She was the first woman in America to earn a first-class glider pilot's license, and one of the few then who became a fully qualified radio operator and navigator. These skills were critical during the survey flights she and my father made all over the globe, charting air routes in the early days of the aviation industry.

My mother never sought any special acclaim for her aviation accomplishments, thinking of them as a necessary part of life with my father, nothing more. Still, some aviation historians believe that Amelia Earhart would not have perished had she possessed the navigation and communications skills of Anne Morrow Lindbergh.

I sat next to Anne Morrow Lindbergh reading my book, while the caregivers cleaned up the kitchen and bedroom and my mother held her mouse. Holding it, she watched me for a while, then put down the mouse and picked up a glass of water. She turned the glass over and poured it on my knee.

I don't care what they say about short-term memory loss. She's been planning that for a week.

It's not that I think she's been plotting against me personally. I was surprised to realize, as I felt the water soak in, that I don't think about these things the way I used to. Even just a few months ago, I would have been upset and tearful, interpreting her action as driven by anger at me. I would imagine that pouring water on me was a deliberate act of punishment because I was reading my book instead of talking to her the way a good daughter would.

Now I think it may have little to do with me, except that I happened to be nearby when she had a water glass and wanted to pour. She may have been feeling itchy and provocative, I could sense that; but it is also true that her thoughts seem to float freely these days, until finally they light on something, whether inside or outside herself, and linger there for a few moments like a butterfly on a blossom. She gets involved with the fire then, or with her own memory, or with something she sees through the window, or with the water in the glass, but it isn't a weighty landing. She's just touching down for a while.

So my theory, since I always have to have a theory, is that she looked at the liquid last night, and maybe the week before, too, during the episode of the grapefruit juice and the lily. She just looked, and what came into her mind as she looked was pouring. Liquids are for pouring. So she poured.

I still jumped, insight notwithstanding, when the first splash hit my blue jeans. But then I put my hand under the flow of water and caught what I could of it. There wasn't much water, maybe half a cup in all. *Go with the flow,* I thought, inanely.

Soon the flow stopped. My hand was dripping, my knee was wet. I looked at my mother. She looked right back at me. I shrugged, got a napkin, and cleaned up.

Meaning can be elusive, but there is sometimes a glimmer of perceptiveness that is oddly reminiscent of her old, intuitive self.

The caregiver Catherine Clark, by her own admission, is a very independent woman, one who is unwilling to surrender much of herself in a relationship with a man. She asked my mother recently, during a mellow evening when several people were gathered in the house, how she should go about approaching "a beloved." I don't know whether Catherine expected an answer, but she got one.

"Well, first you make yourself beautiful," my mother told her. Catherine asked if there was anything else.

"You must bow to him," my mother told her, quite seriously. Later, she said thoughtfully, "I think you should kiss him."

Sometimes the message seems apt, poignant, and personal, then it slips sideways, sliding into something else that is difficult to define. It may be an emanation of neurology gone awry, or maybe it is just a bit of theater. Sometimes Mother will speak for a while in a mysterious foreign language, something that sounds like a mixture of French and Dutch, but is unintelligible to anyone who hears it. And once in a while, I think, her dreams and fears get so mixed up with her daily life that she reacts to them as if to real experiences.

One day, Sue Gilman said, my mother sat in her chair as usual, but she was looking so sad for such a long time that Sue finally sat down beside her to find out what the trouble was.

"Is there something wrong, Mrs. Lindbergh?" Sue asked. "Can I help you?"

"I shot a man," my mother confessed, her voice heavily burdened with consternation and remorse. It took Sue and Karen Frazier together a good hour and a half to convince her that she couldn't possibly have shot a man. She didn't have a gun, and Karen and Sue had both been with her all the time, every day, for a week. It was impossible for her to have done any such thing. All the same, it was difficult for my mother to let go of the idea.

"Maybe they should have just told her he deserved it," my brother Jon said when he called and heard the story. Maybe so. Oh well, next time.

When I left the house last night, after I mopped up the water, Sue Gilman was up with my mother for quite a long time afterward. Close to the end of my visit, my mother was falling asleep in her chair, so Sue helped her into bed after I went home. But she wanted to get right up again. She was very tired, but she couldn't settle in, so Sue got her up, brought her back out to the living room, and they sat and read together. They were looking at a book of large color photographs of "the most beautiful places in the world." Sue was commenting on the sites chosen for inclusion: the Taj Mahal, Mount Kilimanjaro, Haleakala Crater in Maui, a place where my mother and I once hiked together, with Land and his wife and a couple of old friends, more than twenty years ago.

When they had looked at the photographs for a while, Sue asked if my mother thought she might be ready to go to sleep now. My mother turned to Sue and spoke. "I'm near the end of my time," she said slowly and directly. "This means so much to me."

She appeared perfectly willing to go into the bedroom then, and while Sue was helping her into bed, my mother said to her politely, "I can't thank you enough."

Then she said it again, "I can't thank you enough." And then again.

After Sue had said good night and tiptoed out of the room, she could still hear my mother repeating to herself, as if rehearsing a role for which she did not feel quite prepared, "I can't thank you enough . . . I can't thank you enough . . . I can't thank you enough."

8

August 2000

Letter with a Foreign Stamp
It was not fair of you to flaunt your days,
Your scarlet, fluttering days in front of me;
Bright taunting pennants, whipping me to scorn,
Hours of color you mention casually.
Why did you say "It seems like April now—
—Those chestnut trees—" You said, "When I have time
I hunt among the bookstalls on the quai
For old dust-covered leaves of fragrant rhyme."
Why did you say "Last night I wore my shawl
—Mandarin red—I wish you could have seen—
And as I danced the silk fringe caught the light
—Some stranger stopped and murmured 'Rouge de Chine!' "
Oh use bright words with caution, fire is keen:
"Those chestnut trees"—"Some stranger"—"Rouge de
    Chine!"

—Anne Morrow, *The Smith College Monthly*,
    March 1927

It is sunny and hot in Vermont, and my mother wears a purple hat every day. It is not actually purple but lavender. I gave it to her for her birthday this June, a lavender straw hat with a wide, slightly up-curling brim.

This style of hat is very popular now, perhaps because it is both indestructible and festive. Like the traditional panama, it can be rolled or folded into a suitcase, or squashed haphazardly into a raincoat pocket, and emerge again much later with no ill effects. One can tie a flowing chiffon scarf around the crown, say for an outdoor wedding, and achieve a formal, celebratory look. It can be decorated with bows, or pins, or flowers, to fit almost any occasion.

I see these hats everywhere this summer, in all colors, in store windows and in catalogs and on women walking down the street. I bought white ones for myself and my younger daughter Susannah, who is twenty-five and goes to a lot of weddings. My older daughter, Elizabeth, got a wheat-colored one. Lizzy is a teacher and a quilter and tends to prefer natural colors. Her cousin Connie, Anne's daughter, is now an artist living in Brooklyn and should have a bright red hat, but I haven't found one yet. If Anne were still alive, I'd get her one in that shade of deep blue that reminds me of wild blueberries and the waters off the coast of Maine on a chilly day. But for my mother, who has worn lavender all her life, it had to be lavender.

We attached a circle of artificial flowers to the rim of the hat on the afternoon of my mother's birthday. It looked like a crown of daisies, though the flowers were not daisies but plumeria, from Hawaii. They were given to my mother during last year's birthday celebration, when my brother Land, his daughter Erin, and their friend Kristi Hager came for the family gathering. Erin and Kristi showed us all how to dance the

Hawaiian hula and brought with them several Hawaiian leis made of multicolored cloth and silk flowers, to adorn those of us who danced. They also brought this one little crown of white flowers for my mother to wear on her head as she watched her family sway, with varying degrees of grace and credibility, to taped music from the Hawaiian Islands.

The flowers are now on her hat, and they look so real I can almost smell the fragrance of the white plumeria, an extraordinarily beautiful blossom. My mother and father both loved the scent of plumeria; in fact, my mother had a plumeria tree planted close to my father's grave.

The tree itself is just a short and stumpy shrub with thick, misshapen branches, blunted at the ends as if by error or disease. *Leprous*, I thought to myself when I first saw a plumeria shrub. When not in bloom, it looks like every child's nightmare of leprosy. *Everything eaten away except the stumps.* As soon as the flowers appear, however, all else is forgotten in the creamy whiteness of the petals and the heavenly scent.

My mother has taken to picking up her hat and placing it on her head as soon as she is dressed in the morning. She wears it in the house and in the car, and she even walked into the doctor's office with it one afternoon when Ann Cason and I took her there for an appointment.

She laboriously made her way up the steps to the Hitchcock Clinic in Lyndonville holding on to the handrail, with one of us at each elbow and the lavender hat firmly in place. Her head was bent as she took the steps, so that from my position, looking down on her, she appeared frivolous, like an ambulatory flower arrangement that Ann and I were delivering into the old brick building.

We went to see the doctor about her feet. Arthur has been

increasingly concerned because there are more sores and swellings lately, and an ingrown toenail that required a visit to the podiatrist and some minor surgery. Now I can see discoloration at the end of one big toe, an area that has turned purple. It isn't the gentle, ladylike lavender of her hat, either. It's a dark, angry, bruise-colored purple, and it looks painful.

Tim Thompson, the doctor, came into the room where we were waiting, and smiled at us all. Ann and I smiled back, while my mother looked at him regally from under her hat. Tim sat down in a chair facing my mother almost knee to knee, and inspected her toes with the utmost care and gentleness. He then placed his hand on her calf, about halfway between ankle and knee.

"She's thrown a clot," he said to me, looking up into my face seriously. (Thrown a clot? Like a horse throwing a shoe? The phrase was unfamiliar.) "It's a little cholesterol clot, cutting off some of the circulation in the lower part of her foot. Feel her leg here, just below the knee. See how cold that is?"

I crouched and felt, and he was right. The skin below her knee was much colder than the knee itself. It felt like a child's hands when the mittens first come off after a long morning playing outside in the snow. I wanted to rub my mother's skin vigorously and give her hot cocoa.

Tim told us that today's situation was not terribly serious, but we would need to watch carefully for other clots, in effect monitor her circulation. More severe clots could be dangerous, and he said to make absolutely sure that my mother does not wear restrictive shoes, because they can contribute substantially to the problem. He also said, to reassure us, that we would most likely know right away if a more dangerous clot were to develop.

"If she has a significant blockage," he told us, "it will hurt, and she'll let you know." But will she? I looked at my mother, wondering. She looked back. She said nothing.

Tim turned and addressed her directly for the first time. "Do your feet hurt now?"

No answer at all from under the lavender hat. No movement, no change in expression.

"Do they hurt a *little*?" he questioned, leaning forward toward her, smiling.

Nothing.

"Hard to say, hmmm?" Tim said to my mother with a twinkle in his eye.

I laughed, because Tim is always astute and always tactful. "Hard to say" was the perfect thing to say. "Hard to say" is where we live.

On the way home, we stopped at Carmen's, the ice-cream shop in Lyndonville, and I went up to the window and bought a dish of strawberry shortcake with vanilla ice cream for my mother. I asked the server for plenty of whipped cream on it, too. We had just been to the doctor's office, after all.

I bought a second dish for myself and would have treated Ann Cason, too, but she declined. Ann has been following a strict all-protein diet and besides that, she was driving. The strawberry shortcake looked as if it might be very messy, and it was.

My mother and I each held a plastic spoon and a plastic dish, heaped high with strawberries and ice cream and whipped cream. The rich golden cake underneath was soon soaked with strawberry juice, while the melted ice cream ran down into the bottom of the dish and over my fingers on the outside. My mother and I were both loaded with paper napkins, but they didn't do us much good.

We each dug in, and we ate heartily. From the backseat I could see my mother's face in the van's right-side rearview mirror, framed by the lavender hat. Her expression was serious and concentrated, the flowers on her hat were vibrating with the motion of the car, and there was a round dab of vanilla ice cream on her chin all the way home.

That afternoon I began to think about my mother's hat, and about ice cream and strawberries, and then about her toes, which had been regularly cared for and coddled by Arthur and surgically treated by the podiatrist and carefully examined by the doctor, and yet they still looked terrible. It seemed to me wrong that my mother's head should be so flowery and frivolous and carefree while her toes were so bleak and bruised and sad. They received excellent care, but they deserved more than that. They deserved to be celebrated. Her toes should be decorated with something in the nature of a lavender hat with flowers, I thought. And then I had an idea. Why not?

I went up to my mother's house later with a bottle of rose-pink nail polish, which I had bought in honor of the birth of Rose, my niece Wendy Lindbergh's new baby daughter, on August 20 of this year. I had painted my toenails pink for Rose. Now I was determined to paint my mother's as well.

In summer my daughters and I usually paint our toenails, partly because we wear sandals and go barefoot a lot, and partly because Susannah claims that it is impossible to be depressed if you paint your toenails, especially if you paint them bright red. I have tested this theory and have found it to be true, but I was pretty sure that my mother would not put up with bright red toenails. They would make her feel like a painted hussy, which some of us think is the whole point of having red toenails—but not for my mother's generation.

I brought a hand towel and some Q-tips and some polish remover for the mistakes I was sure to make. I thought I would start by massaging my mother's feet with lotion, something Arthur and the caregivers had begun doing regularly, and which Tim approved because it would also discourage the clots.

My mother was sitting in her chair, still in her lavender hat, now wearing soft pink velour pants and a matching top. Her bare feet rested on a fleece rug about the size of a bath mat. It looked like the sheepskin rugs we all ordered for our babies to sleep on back in the 1970s.

When I sat in front of her table and touched her feet, she looked down at me curiously but did not protest. I held one of her bare feet in my hand and thought how sleek and delicate and soft it was, like a shell from the beach, pale to translucency, and rubbed smooth by loving fingers. Like her hands, her feet were thoroughly cared for. They were held gently by family and friends and caregivers, they constantly received attention, they were never taken for granted and never forgotten. In a perfect world, every old person's hands and feet would be treated with such tenderness and touched with such love every day.

But my mother's toenails were terrible! They were yellowed and crusty and pathetic: poor, hard, neglected husks of little-old-lady toenails that only science and medicine ever looked at. What a fate! What a shame! What fun did these toenails ever have? I was saddened at the sight of them, and I went to work immediately.

Stroke by stroke, concentrating hard so that I wouldn't make the mess I usually do with my own, I painted my mother's toenails rose-pink. This was a big surprise to my mother.

At first she was so startled by the feeling of the tiny wet

brush on her big toenail—what was I *doing* down there?—that she jerked her foot away and peered forward over the table, frowning at me. But when I held up the bottle of nail polish with a goofy and hopeful expression on my face, she relaxed and put her foot back again. She leaned over to look as I carefully, slowly brushed on the polish, and she did not withdraw her foot again.

Carefully, deliberately, I covered up the disaster areas until all the yellow was gone. Why should her toes be a disgrace anyway? If her head can be lavender, why can't her toes be rose? Toenail by toenail, I turned them all rose-pink, one, then three, then five, then ten little pink toenails. Beautiful! I was ridiculously pleased with myself when I'd finished.

"There!" I said. "That's much better!" And I kissed her.

My mother made no comment and gave me no hint that she was pleased. By now she was reading again, and she gave me no sign that she noticed what I had done. There was no reaction to the kiss, either. But the next evening when I came up to visit, she was wearing open-toed sandals, and three times, while we sat reading together, I caught her sneaking a look at her feet.

She has had a benevolent look on her face just lately, an interested, unresistant expression, and a kind of openness of feature that is pleasant and companionable. Something has loosened that was tight in her, and I think she may even be enjoying herself, but of course she's not about to say so.

I have noticed that she seems to be involved in conversations, too, in a way that she wasn't a year ago. People have always spoken to her, or asked her questions, or courteously made comments in her direction, even though she rarely responded. But now, quite often, she does respond.

The other day, for instance, Arthur was talking about Bill

Moyers's television series on death and dying, which aired this summer, and about a related program at the Buddhist meditation center. The program is centered around acceptance of one's own death, he said. He asked my mother if she ever thought about such things. Did she ever think about her own death?

"Oh, I'm not going to die for a *very* long time," she told him calmly, with confidence.

I'm beginning to think she's right, and I am surprised to find that I don't mind. I didn't think it would ever happen, but I am growing accustomed to having her alive, not the way she used to be, but exactly as she is. I am beginning to like our life together, right now. I don't understand this at all, but for the time being it makes me happy.

Meanwhile, except for my mother and me, everybody around here is talking about death and dying. Ann Cason also saw the Bill Moyers series. She found it fascinating. "He really covers everything: all points of view on terminal care and the dying process," she said.

We talked about birth and death and care at my mother's house, while my mother read to herself from *The Little Book of Prayers,* an anthology edited by David Schiller for Workman Publishing. Every so often my mother shook the book, shake-shake-shake, because flies kept landing on it. There were hundreds of flies in the house that day.

Ann was talking about Bill Moyers's coverage of "terminal agitation," a term used to describe the excitability and sometimes violent behavior of dying patients. She said this might come as a result of liver failure, or as a side effect from certain pain medications. She said, further, that there was an interest now in what was called "terminal sedation," a euphemism for a kind of drug-induced coma at the very end of life. If I understand this procedure correctly, it is one in which the agitated dying patient is sedated into sleep and essentially sleeps until his or her death.

I didn't know what I thought about this. How was it different from euthanasia, or a Dr. Kevorkian killer cocktail? I wasn't sure I approved.

Shake-shake-shake, went my mother's book. The flies were impossible. I looked around the room. "Don't you guys have a flyswatter?"

I saw, or thought I saw, Ann Cason and Karen Frazier exchanging a glance of concern. Suddenly I remembered. "Oh, boy. You're Buddhists," I said.

Buddhists respect all sentient beings and do not believe in taking life, though not all of them are activists on this subject. In fact, they are not all vegetarians, either. However, most Buddhists I know refrain from taking life if they can.

"No fly swatting, right?" I asked.

Ann giggled. No help from that quarter. I grinned at her and then recalled Susan Drommond, one of our very first Buddhist caregivers from several years ago. Susan is big and beautiful and warmhearted, with long, flowing chestnut curls, and one day she stood blocking the door of my mother's house in Connecticut like a warrior angel, confronting the exterminator.

The poor man was just doing his job. He had come to the house every year from Terminix. It was his annual task to rid my mother's house of all the moths and mites and fleas and gnatlike creatures that take up residence in the cereal boxes of southern Connecticut during the damp and muggy summers. But Susan would have none of it, and she sent him away.

"What are we going to do about this?" Land asked me on the phone afterward. I didn't know. We both visualized a termite invasion, or a battalion of deer ticks bearing Lyme disease, or a flotilla of fleas floating across Long Island Sound like Washington crossing the Delaware. It could be a very difficult summer. Without Susan, however, it would be impossible.

"Let's do nothing," I said, "at least for a while." This is my favorite solution to a lot of problems in the family, and it often works surprisingly well. We skipped Terminix that year, and the house remained standing. My mother doesn't eat cereal anyway, and Land and I just took to bringing our own when we visited.

Shake-shake-shake. Right now my mother was being besieged by flies, and I had to put a stop to it.

"Okay, fine," I said to Ann and Karen. "You're Buddhists. But I'm a Christian, and we kill *everything!*"

I rose from my chair with murder in my eyes, but Ann got up, too. She had another idea. "How about catching them and releasing them outside?" she suggested, and grabbed two blue plastic cups from the counter. Clapping them together like cymbals, she walked around the room.

"Are you kidding?" I said. "Remember sixth-grade science? They have a zillion little eyes! They'll see you coming! You'll never catch them that way."

"What about the vacuum cleaner?" Karen Frazier asked. She had brought it out of the closet. I looked at it, and so did Ann.

"I bet it won't actually kill them," I said.

"Maybe you can let them go outside afterward," said Karen. "We could open the bag."

"Or else just think of it as terminal sedation?" I suggested.

Ann ignored me, plugged in the vacuum cleaner, and turned it on.

She advanced slowly on the flies, one at a time. I could hear a tiny "thwup" as each fly was sucked into the nozzle and toward whatever ultimate fate was waiting for it. I couldn't see my mother, but I knew she was watching. And I heard Ann Cason, my Buddhist friend and my mother's chief caregiver, aiming the vacuum-cleaner nozzle slowly around the living room and muttering "The Terminator" in a hoarse, Arnold Schwarzenegger whisper. It was a wonderful evening.

9

November 2000

Caprice
[Doggerel Written After Seeing Raquel Meller]

"I should like to be a dancer,
A slim persuasive dancer,
A scarlet Spanish dancer,
If you please!"
But he said, "Just now we're crowded
With these Carmens—simply crowded—
I can't find—." His forehead clouded,
"Vacancies."

"I suppose you want to tango,"
And he sighed—"Or a fandango
Scarlet cigarette and tango—
Scarlet smile—
In a century or twenty
We may want you. We have plenty
Just at present—more than plenty
For a while.

"There's a place for Quaker Maidens,
For brown-haired Quaker Maidens,
For blue-eyed Quaker Maidens
There's a place."
So I play the role of Quaker
And I do not blame my maker
For I think I wear the Quaker
With a grace!

But when a tune is tilting,
Like a scarlet skirt is lilting,
That my rebel heart is lilting
No one sees:
"For I want to be a dancer,
A slim, persuasive dancer,
A scarlet, Spanish dancer,
If you please!"

—Anne Morrow, *The Smith College Monthly,*
    October 1926

Another autumn, and my mother and I are both still alive and still together. I can hardly believe it.

This is not what I expected for either one of us. Last year at this time I was sure that she, at least, would be dead by now. A couple of months later, I was less sure. By then, though, I assumed that if she went on living, I would go crazy. I could feel it coming. I just knew that if things continued as they were, I'd either get frantic and flip out, or sink into a severe depression and shut down. One way or the other, out too far or down too deep, I'd be at my wit's end in a year. I would have bet money on it. It's lucky for me that I didn't.

Everything feels different now. Both of us have changed, and I can't tell who has changed the most. I suspect that it's me, because right now I don't see much change in my mother at all, not the way I used to. Maybe that's because sometime over the days and weeks and months we have been together here, I have lost the habit of looking for it.

A year ago, I really thought that every faltering step and every twitch of her hand was a sign of my mother's imminent death. If her face was bloated and pale in the morning, then she'd be gone by nightfall. If there was a gleam of saliva at the corner of her mouth and a rasp in her lungs, I could hear the death rattle in her throat. If she slept most of the night and day and was hard to awaken toward evening, I imagined that this was not sleep but coma.

Lately, day after day and week after week, she has seemed about the same to me. And sometimes when I go up to her house in the evenings, she seems better. I mean that. Quite often she appears in better health and spirits than she has been for many months: more present, more verbal, more focused.

"Is this your dog?" she asked me politely a few nights ago, pointing at Fergus, who was curled up on the rug near her feet.

I was startled by my mother's voice. It was so strong and so engaged, as if she was truly beginning a true conversation. This voice was intimately familiar and yet completely out of context now, eerily reminiscent of her former self, fifteen or twenty years in the past.

Pulling myself together, I responded in the reassuring tones I've adopted since she came to Vermont: "This is *your* dog, Mother. His name is Fergus, and he loves you very much."

She looked at me with bright eyes, skeptically, as if to say, *I know that, you idiot. That's not what I meant at all.*

I wonder how much I have missed over the past year.

Each person who spends time with my mother has a particular and special relationship with her. That is nothing new. She has always conducted her social life on a one-to-one basis. Still, it is interesting to see this happening with her caregivers as well as friends and family. The overall care program proceeds in an integrated and predictable way, as planned, but individual patterns develop, depending on which caregiver is with her. One person will take her for long drives in the countryside and stop for tea at a local restaurant; another stays at home with her and reads poems aloud; a third might concentrate more on music, or personal care, or pay special attention to Fergus. (Susan Shaw bakes homemade dog biscuits, so fragrant as they come out of the oven that it is hard not to grab one and take a bite.)

Laurie Crosby plays word games with my mother, and this is something they both clearly enjoy. A nice aspect of these games is that they do not require conversation, relying instead upon pencil and paper or other simple language aids. Laurie brings magnetic boards with words and letters, or books of simple crossword puzzles and games that can be played in partnership as she and my mother sit side by side.

The last time I was at the house when Laurie was there, she was eager to show me something she and my mother had been working on that day. It was a book of word puzzles in the format of a coloring book for children, very much the kind of thing I used to bring along when traveling for long periods in the car with my two young daughters.

One page had a picture of a pumpkin on it, round and

plump and ready to color. I could imagine small eager fingers clenched around the orange crayon, pressing down hard. Next to the picture, dashes were set next to one another in a line, and some but not all of the letters of "pumpkin" had been printed, like this:

P_ _ _K_N.

"Which letters do you think might go on these lines, Mrs. Lindbergh?" Laurie asked, smiling at Mother, and then at me. Laurie is one of the gentlest people I know, with a quiet sense of humor and a great capacity for patience. She stood in front of my mother's chair, holding the book open directly in front of us, so that my mother could see it and I, from my position on the sofa, could see it as well.

My mother looked up at Laurie.

"How about the first letter? That's already there," Laurie reminded her. "We know what that one is, don't we?"

"P," my mother agreed in her raspy voice, after a long pause.

"What letters could go in those other places, do you think?"

Silence.

"There's the picture, right here." Laurie held the book open with one hand and pointed at the pumpkin with the other. She was standing the way I do when I read stories to the children in a kindergarten class, with the book facing us, not herself. If you do that often enough, you become an expert at reading upside down.

"What do you think that is? What's the word that goes with this picture?"

Still nothing, but I could tell that my mother was participating, at least to some degree. She was looking at Laurie and then at the picture, though her eyes were a little wary and uncommitted. I had the feeling that she might not be in the mood to play this game just now. Maybe she didn't want to play it in my presence. It was an intimate sort of game, a pleasant exercise for one person alone or two people together. With three, perhaps it became awkward and embarrassing, maybe even childish.

Laurie, who like all the caregivers is very sensitive to my mother's moods, started to draw back, probably intending to put the puzzle book aside for the time being.

"*Pignut!*" my mother shouted, in a loud rush of breath. Laurie and I looked at each other, and Laurie's eyes opened wide. She took a breath.

"Pignut, Mrs. Lindbergh?"

"*Yes,*" my mother said. Same emphasis, same decibel level. "*Pignut!*"

I have decided that she has forgotten how to smile, but even so, I think sometimes she's laughing at us all.

The person who has changed most dramatically over the course of the last twelve months is Ben. Taller and broader, he is closer to fourteen than thirteen now, and he moves in a new way. He has a slower swing to his shoulders and a heavier tread with his feet. Not only that; he even sounds different when he walks. If one of the men in my house goes up or down the stairs, I can no longer tell without looking which one it is, my husband or my son. Ben also has the beginnings of a mustache on his upper lip, and his voice often cracks when he speaks or laughs.

Nat says that Ben right now sounds something like the young roosters in the barn. They are just getting big enough to crow this fall, but they haven't quite learned how. Each "cock-

a-doodle-doo" starts out bravely, then breaks off in the middle
and turns back into a baby-bird squawk. There are too many
roosters, in fact, and the little hens that came with them in
the box of baby chicks last spring have yet to lay any eggs. Nat
is a bit disappointed in this particular barnyard project so far,
though he's still holding out some optimism for the future. I
don't want to be a spoilsport, but the future looks dark to me,
literally. We're going into the winter, we haven't seen the sun
for ten days, and hens never lay eggs without light, for no reason that I can understand. Why not? What else is there to do
this time of year?

I was boiling an egg this week while listening to the latest
Florida results of the still-undecided presidential election.
Nat looked over at the bubbling pot I was watching on the
stove. (They do boil, whether you watch them or not, I learned
early on in life.)

"That looks almost like a bantam egg," he said hopefully.

"Except that it came out of the egg carton from the super-
market," I told him, once again dashing his hopes for bantam-
egg production any time soon. I gave up hoping a couple of
weeks ago, which is why I went to the store.

Nat sighed and turned his attention to the news.

"If I could have a bantam egg and a Democratic president,
I'd be perfectly happy," he said.

Don't hold your breath, I thought, equally disillusioned with
poultry and politicians this year. They are what they are, and
that's all there is to it, in my opinion.

Ben, on the other hand, has been enjoying the national elec-
toral crisis, mostly because of the things he hears the news-
casters say, which seem to him both moronic and hilariously
funny. He recited to me on the way to school three different

choice phrases from Dan Rather's election-night coverage on CBS:

- "This race is so close you couldn't slip a cigarette paper between the two candidates."
- "There is so much tension here you can't cut it with a saw: you need a blowtorch."
- "Bush's lead is shakier than cafeteria Jell-O." (my favorite)

My brother Land wasn't sure he would even vote the top of the ticket this year, he was so disgusted with presidential politics. He told me that Montana was going for George Bush by a large margin, so his vote wouldn't make a difference either way. He didn't think he could bring himself to vote for either Bush or Al Gore, let alone Ralph Nader or Pat Buchanan, and said he might just leave that part of the ballot blank.

I haven't talked to him about the election since he was here back in mid-October, so I don't know what he finally decided to do. Land came here for three days to visit our mother, after he had stopped in Connecticut to check on her home there. He brought us artifacts and treasures from the Connecticut house, as he often does: an old family Bible, a slim, bound, and signed edition of a Virginia Woolf essay from our mother's bedroom, and finally a handful of buttons from an old coat that had once belonged to our father. Land found it derelict and tattered and cast aside in an unused bedroom, among other clothes to be given away or taken to the dump.

I put a button in my pocket. I remember the coat very well. It was navy blue, warmly lined, and utilitarian, neither his long, tweedy business overcoat nor his trim military one, but a heavier, shorter, humbler garment with deep pockets for working outdoors. I can see him wearing it on frosty mornings in Connecticut, along with his blue hat with the visor and earflaps, and his heavy work gloves three times the size of my own hand at that time. I see him picking up fallen branches from our woods and dragging them over to a pile he had built for a bonfire, behind the toolshed and as close as possible to the mudflats and tides of Scott's Cove on Long Island Sound.

This must be against all the zoning regulations and environmental codes now, but life in the suburbs was different in the fifties. You could burn things: piles of autumn leaves, garbage, and brush. My father would construct a towering tangle of it all day long, branch upon branch upon branch, until the aggregate was big enough to hide a dozen Brer Rabbits, and taller than any beaver dam I've ever seen. At night, with all of us invited outside in the dark to watch him, he'd pour kerosene on it and throw in a match. Well warned of what was to happen next, we'd all stand back, and the whole mess would burst into flames, a sudden mighty conflagration that burned hot as the fires of hell, bright enough to see by and strong enough to be frightening. I remember flames flickering on the faces of my family and the heat pushing us all back from the fire, firm and inevitable as my father's arm.

I think he liked to instruct us in the inextricable nature of opposites, the thin line between risk and freedom, between danger and safety. Take to the skies in an airplane, but stay clear of the propeller on the ground. Drive off to the far ends of the earth in a Volkswagen, but remember to check the oil and watch the air pressure in the tires, and always look out for the other driver or, as he used to say, "the other damn fool."

In my father's view, a bonfire was both wonderful and terrible. Come out in the night to witness the magnificence of nature, he seemed to be telling us. Come close, look carefully, see and understand the element Fire. And at the same time, watch out! Stand back! Be alert and careful! Learn not to be consumed by flames.

My mother left the button from her husband's overcoat on her table, next to the dish of stones. I saw it there when I came to sit with her one afternoon this week, arriving a few hours earlier than usual because I planned to go out in the evening.

Arthur was at the house, tending to her toes. Most of the summer's nail polish had worn off, and some of the nails were getting long. I sat quietly on the sofa, flipping through a holiday catalog, so as not to be a distraction while Arthur did his work.

He told my mother that he was going to soak her feet in a warm tub of water for a little while, then trim her toenails. She looked at him stonily but did not seem to mind the soaking, as long as that was all that was going on. The trimming, after Arthur had taken the tub away and gently dried her feet, was another matter.

Arthur was sitting cross-legged on the floor facing my mother, on the other side of her table. He moved the table slightly to one side and began his work by taking one of her feet in his hand. She withdrew it immediately, pulling back as if he'd tickled her.

"It's okay, Mrs. Lindbergh," he said, looking up with a mild and patient expression and a lock of hair falling over one eye. "I'm just trimming your nails."

"That big toe looks like it could be scratchy," I suggested helpfully. "You don't want to scratch yourself in your sleep, Mother. You'd hate that. That happens to me sometimes, and it hurts." I put the catalog down and leaned forward to be part of the process. My mother did not acknowledge my presence. Arthur kept looking at her. He smiled.

"We've done this before, Mrs. Lindbergh, haven't we? It's okay," he said. He picked up her foot again. She removed it even faster—removed both feet, in fact, and tucked them as far back under her chair as possible.

"Awww," said Arthur, in crestfallen tones, like a teenager in an old situation comedy. *Leave It to Beaver,* maybe: "Aww, gee, Mom . . ."

"Aww, Mrs. Lindbergh. Don't be that way . . . here, just a minute . . ." He reached up to the arm of the sofa and took the catalog I had put down there. "This sometimes helps," he said to me, handing the catalog to my mother. She rolled it slightly and rapped him on the head.

"Hey!" I began, but Arthur quietly interrupted me.

"No, no. It's fine. It makes it easier for her, and I really don't mind," he explained.

And so it went. Arthur trimmed my mother's toenails while she bopped him on the head. She didn't do it very hard, and she didn't do it the whole time, only when he was working on a particularly hard or tenacious nail. The gesture was almost regal. *I dub thee Sir Arthur, Knight of the Protested Pedicure.* He clipped, she bopped, I watched.

"It's sort of like a blessing," he told me, smiling, when he was through and gathering his things. I shook my head. Buddhists!

"You're amazing," I said.

He smiled again. "Well," he said, "I don't know. This is my third lady of the day, and one of them wouldn't let me touch her feet at all." He looked at my mother's feet, now peacefully resting on the sheepskin under the table, and said reflectively, "That was my thirtieth toenail."

I generally enjoy my mother's forms of protest now. They are unexpected and often delightful. Catherine Clark told me yesterday that when she tried to get my mother up the other day, after all night and a good part of the morning in bed, my mother asked her why it was necessary.

"Why do I have to get up?" she asked, which seemed to Catherine a reasonable question. She explained that it was not good for my mother's circulation to be in one position for such a long time, that she needed to get up and move around a bit for her own health.

"I don't want to interrupt the dancing!" my mother told her. It reminded me of something Ben used to say about his cousin from Brazil, who would converse happily in Portuguese while he and she were playing together: "I don't understand what she's saying, but I know what she means."

Language is limited at the best of times. What really goes on in this world is beyond words, and the truth of it, whatever that is, comes through to us in mystery, always taking its own sweet time.

Last night the Florida Supreme Court unanimously ruled that the secretary of state could not, or not yet, certify the vote count that would have put a Republican president in the White House. And this morning, going out early to feed the chickens, I found a bantam egg.

10

December 2000

Success
I lit the candles in my heart
*   And opened wide the door.*
"And are you she they call 'Success'?
*   Have we not met before?"*

"It seems . . . but no . . . could I forget
*   Beauty so like a star?*
Come, here is bread and here is wine
*   For you have travelled far."*

"Child, I have been here every day.
*   You would not turn or rise*
But called me 'Failure,' seeing me
*   Through tears within your eyes."*

—Anne Morrow, class of 1924, *The Wheel*,
Miss Chapin's School, March 1924

Oh, well. As I told my husband, you can't have everything.
There will be a Republican president, following an election

process that I thought was much more interesting, frankly, than either of the candidates. But the bantam hens are still going strong, and so is my mother.

I am seeing her in a new way this winter. I see her as she is just at the moment. I think I have dropped my habitual lens of bereaved, aggrieved interpretation, almost without noticing that I have done so. Suddenly it seems enough for me just to see her from day to day, and it does not feel so important to think about what I am seeing in her, or noticing about her. I'm not even sure that I am capable of analysis anymore where my mother is concerned. Because I see this way, nakedly, observing my mother without the usual internal commentary, something that used to separate us has dissolved. It is as if the cluttered furniture of my own thoughts has been pushed back against the walls of our relationship. All at once there is room to move freely again. There may even be enough room to dance.

I was surprised last month when Land told me that on his last visit, our mother's skin tone appeared changed to him. He said her face had a completely different quality, her skin had become "waxy and transparent," and he wondered what that meant. I didn't know. I can't see the quality he described at all. I can just see her face itself, soft as petals and pale as parchment. I don't see "deterioration," or "progression," or "signs" of one thing or another, although I used to see all those things and more. Now I can't see changes, and I can't summon any words. I see only her face.

On the other hand, I also have begun thinking about her at all periods of her life. I like imagining her at seventeen, at twenty-five, at forty-one, and at my age, fifty-five. I find myself looking back over her whole lifetime of writings, her books and her diaries, even her very earliest published poems in the magazines from her school and college. I am so grateful that these have been saved, and I am amused to notice in the school publications from Miss Chapin's or Smith College that she often penciled angry comments to herself in the margins, next to her own published work. There are light editorial self-scoldings like "I can't bear to read this!" or "Clumsy!" I have done the same thing, and it makes me smile to know it is something we share.

There is snow on the farm, more than there was last year at this time. Everywhere I look, the background is white. There is so little differentiation between earth and sky that it is hard to tell where one stops and the other begins as I move across our pasture on cross-country skis and stop to take in the landscape around me. I can see our house and barn, then up the road my mother's little house, looking more than ever like a Swiss chalet at this season. She must be sitting in her chair in front of the fire. There is smoke curling up from her chimney.

I can't see many details in the snowy landscape. The sheep in our barnyard are visible from this distance only because they have black faces and black feet. I know that when I make my final descent, they will follow me along the fence in a watchful woolly mob, galloping together in slow motion right up against the woven wire of their enclosure as I ski past them. They won't take their eyes off me until I leave the trail that skirts the barnyard, and branch off toward the house. Why do they do this? Do they think I have grain for them in the pockets of my parka—skiing shepherd? Only in your dreams, sheep.

We have fewer sheep than we did a month ago, because Nat and I took five of them in the back of his new red truck down to Ascutney, Vermont, to sell to a man named Bill Yates. At first I misunderstood and thought Nat had said "Bill Gates," and wondered very briefly if the Microsoft billionaire had diversified into sheep farming in Vermont—not an astute financial move—but instead it was Yates, a farmer about our own age, recommended by a sheep-owner friend of ours from East Burke who has had long-term dealings with him.

Nat woke up early that day, looked out the window behind our bed, and swore. ("F—ing wind, f—ing sheep.") He was anticipating bad weather and bad behavior both. It was cold and blustery, so he was sure that the animals would be skittish, making them that much harder to load into the pickup. He was already dreading this job.

When the time came, they were in fact quite docile, but Nat discovered he would have to remove the truck's tailgate temporarily in order to back the vehicle up to the barn. The tailgate would not hold the weight of the animals, and we did not have a ramp. ("F—ing truck.") Then he would need to load the sheep and get the tailgate back on very quickly so the animals would not try to jump out.

Tailgate removed, my husband coaxed the sheep out of their stall with a bucket of grain, while I waited in a quiet, nonthreatening manner in the shadows, holding a cobweb-covered wooden shutter. It came from a pile of shutters stacked in the back of the barn since whichever previous owner of the farm had removed them from the farmhouse windows, probably in order to paint the house. Nobody had ever put the shutters back on the windows, but they came in handy for other purposes. I was on the alert with mine, gripping it crosswise, poised to encourage the sheep from behind should they prove reluctant to move toward the truck and try instead to scatter mindlessly throughout the barn, bleating and stumbling in their characteristic infuriating way.

Luckily, they left their stall in one mass, as sheep will sometimes do, then surged around the inner passages of the barn, pushing heavily past an abandoned rabbit cage and overturning an old western saddle. They startled themselves into confusion by banging into a barrel, but then they regrouped and followed Nat and the bucket of grain—I think they would follow him over a cliff if he went over first with the bucket—right into the back of the truck. I then ran up behind them with my shutter and shoved it firmly against the back of the pickup in case the flock should have second thoughts while Nat was replacing the tailgate.

It was a tricky process, and we were all still nervous as we traveled over the local dirt roads toward Vermont Route 5, which would take us south along the Connecticut River and the railroad tracks. Nat did not want to try the much faster Interstate 91, though it ran parallel to our planned route, because we weren't sure what the sheep would do on the highway. This was the first time we had used this truck, bought last summer, to transport animals. As we rolled down our long hill heading for Route 5, the cargo was swaying and bleating behind us, and Nat was still mumbling imprecations up front.

Route 5, however, is one of our favorite roads, a beautiful drive through villages and farm meadows, bordering some of the prettiest parts of the river, with generous winding curves of shining water rimmed with ice and overhung with willow, an occasional hawk perching on a high pine branch where the woods meet the shoreline, and flocks of shorebirds, ducks and migrant geese, resting on the sandbars. We got progressively cheerier as we made our way through Passumpsic and East Barnet and Barnet and McIndoes Falls without incident. By the time we got to Wells River, the sheep were quiet, and Nat had begun to relax.

"It's great to see those tracks so well polished, isn't it?" he said, glancing over at the railroad line running beside us. I had a quick irreverent image of French maids with feather dusters, but Nat was talking, of course, about increased rail traffic on this line. Vermont is making a concerted effort to bring back rail travel, and this, along with the sensible use and preservation of the Connecticut River itself, is a project very dear to Nat's heart. He has served on the New Hampshire–Vermont Joint Commission on the Connecticut River for many years, currently as its chairman, but he has no official railroad capacity.

Nonetheless, he is very well informed and was asked to testify in the Vermont senate when the state was working on a plan to buy the Boston and Maine line from Timothy Mellon, a young man of means who had acquired the railroad but was not, in the opinion of those in the know, taking proper care of it. Because the Mellon family was of old moneyed stock, and long known to my mother's family, the Morrows, I often thought that the simplest solution to the Timothy Mellon problem would have been for my mother to write a polite little note to his mother, asking her to remind her son to pay more attention to his trains. Nobody listened to me, but the fact is, motherhood is much more powerful than politics and always was.

Nothing makes Nat happier than talking about railroads, and I love to listen to him, not only because of his enthusiasm but also because I like all the railroad names. I remember when my brother Land used to play and sing railroad songs on his guitar, especially "The Wabash Cannonball," the most haunting train song of all. I also loved the wide variety of railroad ballads in *The Fireside Book of Folk Songs*, a family treasure from my Lindbergh childhood.

I still have the songbook and keep it by the piano in Vermont, tattered but complete. It includes a carbon copy, stuffed into the back pages of the songbook and labeled "Scott's Cove, December 25, 1959," of my father's typed recollection of all the verses he could remember to the song he knew as "Abdul Abulbul Amir." My favorite verse of that grisly ballad about two mutually destructive warriors was the one about Abdul's rival, Ivan Skavinsky Skavar. According to my father's version, Ivan "could imitate Irving, play poker and pool, / And strum on the Spanish guitar," all of which sounded wonderfully debonair and dissolute, except that I didn't know who or what Irving was.

It was a very pleasant drive, all in all, the day we shipped the sheep. We got to Ascutney and unloaded them at Bill Yates's farm with no mishaps, thanks to Bill himself and to his dark-haired and lovely college-age daughter, who left a copy of Mary Karr's *The Liars' Club* open facedown on the kitchen table while she came out to help us with the animals. She told us there was a new kitten in the hayloft, and I noticed while I was in the kitchen that I could see a donkey through the kitchen window, out in the pasture with the cows, and that there were a couple of freshly emptied milk bottles with calf nipples on them, sitting in the kitchen sink. It was a busy place on a Sunday afternoon.

On the way home, Nat showed me the check he got from Bill Yates for the sheep, made out for $360. After that he spoke at some length about the spiritual values of country life, as we have lived it these past thirty years since we both moved to Vermont in the late 1960s.

I was partly listening and partly humming under my breath: " 'She's long and tall and handsome / And loved by one and all / She's a modern combination / Called the Wabash Cannonball.' "

For me, December begins a quieter time that lasts for most of the three coldest months of our winter. I'll be glad to settle down. I have traveled a great deal this past year, going to schools and bookstores and conferences and libraries in connection with my work, as well as traveling for family and other business. I've been involved in dozens of programs in dozens of states all over the country, and quite a few local ones as well. Most often I am invited to schools and libraries, but sometimes I end up at an air force base or a community center, usually in connection with the family history.

My final program of this year took place at the VFW hall in Lyndonville, Vermont, on a Saturday evening in the middle of December.

I had been invited by Lieutenant Colonel Madeleine Batten, the first woman ever to head the Vermont National Guard. It was a holiday program including an awards ceremony for a group of young people in a local Civil Air Patrol program, and for their families. Lieutenant Colonel Batten, whom I had not met yet, had asked me to help present a Lindbergh Award for individual achievement.

Everybody at the VFW hall was either in uniform or in blue jeans and a sweatshirt, which made the occasion seem formal and informal at the same time. Little girls ran back and forth from table to table in ponytails and pink sneakers, while young members of the Civil Air Patrol squadron, male and female, stood patriotically silent near the Vermont and American flags. They presented the colors, received their awards, marched and saluted with dignity and precision, while the audience of siblings and parents and grandparents applauded enthusiastically.

It was hard at first to get a sense of the event but it felt to me like some mixture of church supper, community meeting, and graduation ceremony. The families had been invited to watch and support the program but were not participants, and were therefore not required to dress up. The children, at least those involved in the Civil Air Patrol, were uniformed and polished and solemn, with perfect posture and respectful bearing. I was escorted to my seat by a handsome young cadet about seventeen years old, one of the oldest in the group of young people whose ages ranged from eleven to twenty-one, in fact the very same Sergeant Chris Westover to whom I later presented the Lindbergh Award.

I sat with the dignitaries at a long head table covered with a white tablecloth, between Lieutenant Colonel Batten on my right and another uniformed officer, whose name card said "Col. James D. Rowell," on my left. Directly behind us there was a platform with a live DJ playing Christmas CDs on an elaborate sound system. The music could be heard throughout the hall, and as I sat down, I could hear Colonel Rowell singing along in deep, rich undertones: " 'Sleigh bells ring, are you listening . . . ' "

Lieutenant Colonel Batten herself turned out to be a short, sturdy, and very merry white-haired woman, accompanied by a thin sinewy white-haired husband with a bushy mustache and a big grin. He is also a Lieutenant Colonel Batten, and he introduced the head table. Our speaker was Lieutenant Catherine Wood, who serves as the squadron chaplain. Before the dinner she was sitting quietly at her place, stitching away with a needle and what looked like embroidery thread, work-

ing on purple crosses for little white pockets, like keys in decorative key-holders, in her lap. She gave both the invocation at
the beginning of the program and a talk, halfway through, on
"My Life in China."

Lieutenant Wood grew up as a missionary's daughter in the
Far East with her parents and her brother, "bringing Jesus to
the Communists," as she told us. She continues to work in a
missionary capacity with prisoners at our local correctional
center who, she said softly, and with a kind of sad awe, "never
knew Jesus. Can you believe that?" Lieutenant Wood, like
Lieutenant Colonel Batten, is silver-haired but with a
rounded, Mrs. Claus look, and a gentle uncomplicated devo-
tion characterizing her faith.

It was clear to me that her Jesus was the one of my childhood: blue-eyed and surrounded by lambs and children, with
nothing but love and forgiveness in his message. She spoke,
too, of her worries about the great Yangtze River, "with all the
dams they have now," and she spent some time recalling the
terrible floods in China during her time there.

I thought at once of my young parents, flying into China in
the seaplane *Tingmissartoq*, the Lockheed Sirius, in the
1930s, bringing relief supplies to Chinese citizens in disaster
areas when the Yangtze was in full flood. My mother was not
yet thirty at the time, and she weighed just over a hundred
pounds. She told her children years later that some of the people she and my father had come to help were so desperate that
they tried to climb on board the seaplane, masses of them, almost swamping the Sirius in the dark and flooded waters of
their drowning country. Once, she said, my father had to hold
a group off the plane with a loaded pistol. I knew he was an expert marksman, and her story left me with a grim vision of my
father, pointing a gun with one deadly-accurate hand at a

teeming group of frantic and disorderly people to whom he was delivering relief supplies, life itself, with the other hand.

Madeleine, as I quickly began to think of Lieutenant Colonel Batten while we were getting acquainted over dinner, confided that she had stayed up late the night before, making 123 tiny high-winged monoplanes, one for each place at each table. These looked very much like my father's *Spirit of St. Louis,* only these were rendered in chewing gum (wings), peppermint LifeSavers (wheels), toothpicks (propeller), and Smarties (these were for the body of the airplane, each a compact cylinder of hard candy like a roll of nickels, slanting from cockpit to tail).

My airplane was made with a stick of Wrigley's spearmint gum; Colonel Rowell's had Big Red; and Madeleine's was Doublemint. During a lull in the program, while some of the participants were organizing themselves for the next event, I took out a pen and wrote "NX-211," the call letters for the *Spirit of St. Louis,* on as many chewing-gum wings as I could reach from where I sat. On behalf of both my family and my community, during the holiday season, it seemed to me this was the very least I could do.

11

January 2001

When we start at the center of ourselves, we discover something worthwhile extending toward the periphery of the circle. We find again some of the joy in the now, some of the peace in the here, some of the love in me and thee which go to make up the kingdom of heaven on earth.

The waves echo behind me. Patience—Faith—Openness, is what the sea has to teach. Simplicity—Solitude—Intermittency. . . . But there are other beaches to explore. There are more shells to find. This is only a beginning.

—Anne Morrow Lindbergh, *Gift from the Sea*, 1955

A *lot of people* in our family visit the farm for holidays. It feels like a holiday spot, an "over the river and through the woods" destination, where the visitor drives around the last corner at the end of a long dirt road marked with potholes and lined with birch and maple, and suddenly, just at the place where my mother's house is perched on a rise to the left of the road, the whole landscape opens up into a valley farm. This is a small bowl of land, its own world, with its pastures and its hayfields, the big barn and our farmhouse set right at the bottom of the bowl, and a brook running on either side of the buildings.

The houses have a relationship that I like. They seem to affirm and reflect each other across the landscape. We can look up the valley from the farmhouse and see my mother's light in her bedroom window at night, she can look down from her height of land and see our family and animal activities by day. Years ago, while we were walking the property to establish the site for her house, she said that this farm was held by the valley benevolently, as if cupped in a comforting hand.

Nat's mother and his two older boys came to be with us for Thanksgiving, and my brother Jon and his wife came for a few days afterward. Jon's daughter, Wendy, had visited just a week earlier, with baby Rose and Rose's dad, Hector McDonnell, as well as Wendy's son Sasha Kleszy by her former marriage, a boy who is now seven and has spent many holidays with us. One year, at Easter, our bottle lamb of that season took a great liking to him as a creature about the same size and speed as itself. The lamb, like Mary's in the song, followed Sasha everywhere, very fast. Together they raced around the barn and the lawn, and often through our house as well, with the lamb's little hooves going clickety-clack on the worn wooden floors as it ran full-tilt through the kitchen and the living room, determined to keep up with the running, laughing child.

This Christmas, my own two daughters and my sister's children were home, along with my brother Scott and his family from Brazil. Scott's family has spent many vacations with us over the past decade, but they had not been here in a year and a half. The grandmother on the other side of the family was quite ill for a long period in Brazil, and she died this fall. Raquel, my Brazilian sister-in-law, is quieter and sadder than usual, but the whole family has made the most of the Vermont winter. Brian and Sarah, Ben's Brazilian cousins, especially love the snow.

Over the school vacation, the snow accumulation was steady, and it got deep enough that the children were out every day, cross-country skiing and sledding and building snow forts. We took a carload of them to Burke Mountain, our local ski area, and there Scott and his children, as well as Ben and a couple of friends, went snow-boarding. Brian and Sarah loved this most of all, though none of us had ever tried it before. Brian had been "sand-boarding" in Brazil, which he explained as similar but not identical, and not easily translatable into a winter sport. My fifty-eight-year-old brother, whom I remembered as being an expert skier during his youth, suffered a day of falls, bumps, and bruises before becoming as adept as his two children on a snowboard. He wore a blue and white hat with a tassel that flew behind him when he was speeding across the slopes and flopped in his face when he fell.

At night we gathered at one of the three family houses: our farmhouse, my mother's little chalet, or the cabin about two miles away that my sister once lived in, which is now owned by Marek and Connie, her son and daughter.

My mother perked up during the holiday celebrations, looking alert and interested when people arrived to visit her each day. She is always very much included in family activities, at least the indoor ones, and because she has the hardest time moving from house to house, most of the dinners were at her house. The caregivers, accustomed to cooking for just one or two people, nonetheless produced big meals for the family, and we all helped when we could. Ruth and Marco, our summer gardeners, came back to cook a couple of times on weekends; Marco is an excellent cook as well as an artist and a gardener, and Ruth has been working for a new Internet café that just opened in St. Johnsbury, with three computers, a bunch of tables, and some of Marco's paintings on the walls.

On Christmas Eve, everyone came down the hill to our house for a bountiful supper cooked by Nat, the chef in our family, and we all sang carols afterward by the fire. My mother felt strong enough to walk to our house that night, and she came again for the big midafternoon Christmas dinner the next day.

On Christmas Day, I received an envelope with her handwriting on it, addressed to me. Inside there was a message written on a Christmas card, in her wobbly but unmistakable script. It said, "I deeply appreciate all you have given me."

Tears sprang to my eyes. I turned to Laurie Crosby, who was with my mother for the holiday. Laurie nodded.

"She wrote these herself. Nobody chose the words for her," she said.

Nat opened his card from my mother and showed it to me. He was very touched. It said, in the same hand, "I deeply appreciate all that you do for me."

I began to have the feeling that my mother, once the words were chosen, was on a roll.

Ben's card said simply, "I deeply appreciate you." There was money in it.

"Thank you, Grannymouse," he said, and, "Merry Christmas." He looked over at her shyly, she looked right back. That was all that passed between my mother and my son on Christmas Day. It was enough. I am so glad that they have had time together, that they have gotten used to each other. I have come to realize that this in itself is a form of love.

There were so many meals and so many people over the holidays that I wondered if it sometimes overwhelmed Mother, whether she could express that feeling or not. We all moved in and out of her house through the days in waves of children and dogs and snowy boots and noise. One night Scott and Raquel made a big fondue dinner there for everybody, with salad and dessert and a special pâté that Raquel had planned but for which we had trouble finding the right ingredients and the correct technology, hard as we tried.

"Do you have cognac?" Raquel asked. Her Portuguese accent and tone are both richly musical, her voice quiet and deep. When she speaks, the words sound peaceful, the world seems well ordered. *Surely we must have cognac,* I thought.

We did not have cognac, but somebody remembered seeing a bottle of it at Marek and Connie's house, so Scott drove over there and returned soon, reporting success. He had found both the cognac for the pâté and the kirsch for the fondue, he said.

I questioned him. I had forgotten that kirsch was a component of fondue, a dish I have eaten only in Switzerland. Pouring kirsch into a hot cheese sauce seems more like something a French person would do than a Swiss. Scott, however, insisted that kirsch was a classic element in Swiss fondue and essential for this meal.

I didn't argue. Scott has lived in foreign countries since he was seventeen years old: first in Switzerland, then in England, then in France, and finally in Brazil, and he speaks three or four languages fluently, although I like to tell him that English is no longer one of them. The fact is, he can still speak his native tongue, but as a friend observed, he speaks it like a second language. Although his vocabulary is extensive and he uses words well, he forgets many common English idioms and pronunciations. For example, when he uses a word like "stymied" in conversation (and he does), it rhymes with "pie-eyed," and he's apt to talk about "a good round meal" instead of a square one. Conversations with Scott over the years have made me realize how miraculous, and how ridiculous, any language can be.

Anyway, I wasn't about to complain. He was cooking, and he was driving, and it was a snowy night. One of Nat's "storm of the century" blizzards was in progress, the kind of weather in which Nat paces the floors, plows the driveways, and stocks the shelves with provisions just in case we get snowbound until March. Nonetheless, Scott made it to the cabin and back in his rented vehicle a second time, bearing the needed ingredients.

Cognac, however, was not the last ingredient needed.

"Do you have cornstarch?"

I did have cornstarch, lots of it, because my daughter Susannah had been making serial apple pies. She made three of them during the holidays: one for her father's Christmas present, one for her uncle Ned Perrin's Christmas present, and finally one for her uncle Scott, who said wistfully after the second pie came out of the oven and passed him on its fragrant way to another man, "I'm an uncle, too . . ."

I went down to the farmhouse and came back with the cornstarch for Raquel, but while I was away, something very bad was happening to my mother's blender. It stopped blending, I was told when I returned, and it started smoking. It did not, apparently, handle pâté ingredients well, cognac notwithstanding. Poor Raquel!

"Do you have Cuisinart?" asked my sister-in-law then, still wearily hopeful.

I did not, but Scott had noticed a Cuisinart at Connie and Marek's house while he was looking for the cognac, so he went off through the storm again to get it.

While all the pieces of this dinner were being assembled, and all the people were going in and out of her house, my mother was sitting in her chair, looking at the fire and doing a strange thing with her hands. Every so often she would hold both of them straight out in front of her, palms up, as if to hold off an oncoming vehicle. *That's far enough. Don't come any closer!* Then she would put her palms down, and a moment later, up again. Palms up, *stop that truck,* palms down, palms up again.

I remarked on this to the people around me, as we all worked on the dinner. I was watching my mother while at the same time chopping cheese in the kitchen. I had made bite-size cubes of Gruyère and cheddar, and had a big pile of them in front of me on the counter. (Scott says that for really good fondue, you need Emmentaler cheese as well, but none of us could find it in the stores.)

After following my glance, Laurie told me that she thought our mother was practicing some new exercises the physical therapist had given her during their last session together. Scott commented that the gesture was truly fascinating, because it was in itself a traditional and ancient one, common to many tribal cultures and associated with receiving spiritual messages.

Laurie went over to talk to our mother while the rest of us made the fondue and chattered and laughed, and the children ran in and out of the house, and the dogs scratched on the door to come in or go out, and the snow blew all around us outside. My mother sat still in the midst of the activity, and she listened to Laurie, but she kept on moving her hands. Palms up, palms down, palms up, palms down. I watched her for a long time out of the corner of my eye as I worked, and I still think she was trying to stop a truck.

My mother's resistance to circumstances beyond her control has always been subtle, manifesting itself in interesting ways. My father used to say, long ago, "Your mother devastates with silence," which is perhaps even more true of her now than it was in his time, because she is so much more silent now. But it was true then, too, and I can recall what an effective weapon her silence was against his sudden tirades of opinion and mood. I remember well those times when he moved through the house like a strong wind, shattering everybody else's peace and concentration. It wasn't necessarily a matter of his being in bad humor, it was just that he was so much bigger, so much more energetic, and so much more active than anyone else we knew.

When he was walking and talking and moving around, our father sucked up all the space in his vicinity like some kind of whirlwind, sometimes benign, sometimes ill-boding. If he was indeed angry over something his children had done or, more likely, had neglected to do, the atmosphere was then twice as electric and doubly powerful, the house itself shaking with what my sister used to call "Ambulatory Wrath of God."

If we could do it, we children would scatter out and away from the force like dry leaves before a hurricane. But our mother would remain silent, resting in her own silence, and sooner or later, our father would laugh ruefully, as if to acknowledge that she'd won.

He was to utter the phrase again and again throughout my childhood: "Your mother devastates with silence." I think he was right, she did, and I think it surprised him at first that she could. But later I believe he knew the truth, this strong man who was my father. He recognized that his wife—who was small and subtle, his wife, who always claimed shyness and inferiority and stood quietly in the lee of those great gusts of his traditional, celebrated masculine strength—was by far the stronger of the two.

Sue Gilman told me a couple of days ago that my mother seemed to be getting pretty tired of taking her medicine, and Sue couldn't blame her. Because she can't swallow capsules easily, she gets each dosage in applesauce, several times a day.

"If you think about it, why would anyone want to eat that much applesauce, with or without the medicine?" Sue asked reasonably. What she really wanted to tell me, though, was what my mother had said when she took a particularly distasteful spoonful.

She grimaced, then spoke forcefully. "My husband would not allow this in his house!"

How much he would love to know that she used the memory of his power to express her own feelings, for once, at the end of her life. I think he would throw back his head and laugh out loud with pleasure.

When I am with Scott, or any of my brothers, for any length of time, we do what I call "talking Lindbergh." This doesn't take up too much of a family visit, but it happens at least once or twice during our time together. Talking Lindbergh means that we remember our father and mother as we knew them privately, and we discuss any recent developments on the public, "famous" side of their lives. There are always new books or television programs coming out about our parents, new requests for permission to reprint quotes from their writing or to rename a building or an airfield in their name, and new approaches, every year, by the various "Pretenders," as my sister used to call them, the score of people still believing they are our brother Charles, who died in 1932.

Often there are messages from the Pretenders during the holidays; I suppose because this is a time everyone's thoughts turn to family matters, real and imagined. We get cards and letters, typed pleas for recognition, vaguely threatening letters from questionable attorneys, and requests for DNA testing. My friend and literary agent, Rhoda Weyr, told me she once received in the mail a piece of saran wrap containing a smear of dried blood and a request that she forward this material to me for analysis.

Some of my brothers get angry on behalf of our mother—hasn't she suffered enough?—and I understand their feelings, though I think she was always compassionate about the Pretenders, and is now beyond being hurt by them. Still, I lost a child about the same age as our dead brother, and if dozens of men approached me years later, each one claiming to be Jonathan, I can't imagine how I'd feel.

These days, though, I get most upset by a sense that the men themselves are being exploited, sometimes by their own representatives, sometimes by the news media. They have to be in their seventies by now, if they really believe they are my brother, and it appalls me that they spend their time and resources in this way, rather than on their own lives and their own families.

Friends have asked me why we don't just "settle it for once and for all" by doing our own DNA testing, but the issue is much more complicated. First, we cannot possibly respond to all the Pretenders because there have been too many of them, literally hundreds over the years. Where would we start? When would we stop? We can't agree to DNA testing for the same reason: it would never stop, and I doubt it would convince them anyway. The Pretenders generally disregard all scientific evidence. One of them, however—a relatively recent claimant—dropped his claim last year after comparing his DNA with that of his own niece and finding that it matched.

What appalls me most of all is the truth, which is this: our brother Charles, solely because he was a child of famous parents, died during a botched kidnapping when he was not yet two years old. His dead body was later found and identified by family members, medical authorities, and police forensics, with those findings scientifically reconfirmed several times during the years that followed his death.

There is no mystery here, no long-lost son and heir, no romance. This is not a story. This is the truth, and if I think about it for any length of time, it becomes almost unbearable. A sixteen-month-old child from my own family died for no reason except that somebody wanted money from his parents. This fact alone is horrible enough. To translate such a truth into the lingering spectacle it has become in certain quarters is a travesty. It amazes me sometimes that my family was so intimately linked with both the best and the worst aspects of American culture, and of human nature, for most of a century.

My favorite suggestion for dealing with the many people who claim they are Charles and Anne Lindbergh's first child came from my cousin Faith Morrow Williams. "Why don't you just have a bunch of T-shirts made up?" she said to me once. "Give one to each of them, as a kind of consolation prize. The shirts could have something printed on them like 'I Was the Lindbergh Baby, and All I Got Was This Lousy T-shirt.' " Why didn't I think of this?

After three weeks here with us, Scott and his family returned to Brazil, and I began going up to my mother's house alone in the evenings again. Since I have been reading her poems and her other writings to myself lately, it occurred to me that she might like to hear her own work read aloud. On the other hand, she might not, so I asked her. "How long is it since you've read *Gift from the Sea*, Mother?"

She did not reply, so I suggested that I might read it out loud to her.

There was no answer, no flicker of response, even when I leaned toward her chair and into her face and kissed her and said, "You don't have to listen to this if you don't want to, Mother."

I took silence for assent and started to read:

> *I began these pages for myself, in order to think out my own particular pattern of living, my own individual balance of life, work, and human relationships. And since I think best with a pencil in my hand, I started naturally to write . . .*

I looked over at my mother and asked her if I should stop now or read a little more. She had just had her dinner placed in front of her on her table. It was a mix of pureed vegetables and pureed mashed potatoes and crab cakes, also pureed. She did not look at it, but at me and the book.

"More," she said in her hoarsest whisper, so I went on reading. I finished the first brief section, and when I was almost to the end, I realized that she had not picked up her fork at all. She had not taken a bite of her food. I read the last words on the page, " 'One should lie empty, open, choiceless as a beach—waiting for a gift from the sea.' " Then I picked up her fork myself, reached over to her plate to fill it, and gently popped a bite of crab cake in her mouth.

Then I read, and read, and read some more. I read for fifty-eight pages, but she said nothing. Once in a while I stopped and gave her a bit of vegetable or potato or crab cake, then a sip of water, then I read on.

I don't know what she thought as she listened, but for me

every page was a joy to read because of her attention and the quality of her presence. She was not distracted or in another realm. She was right there with me. I even felt as if *she* were reading to *me,* not the other way around. I could almost hear her voice, her old voice, in my own. Maybe I was unconsciously copying it from memory; I don't know. Or maybe our voices are similar enough that the words, hers and mine together, blend them into one. But it wasn't just me reading. We were reading together.

At the very end of my reading, she leaned toward me, and she said in a wondering way, "But don't you miss your friends?" Her voice was not hoarse then, it was very quiet. She was not as attentive to me, or to the book, as she had been just a minute earlier. I said yes, I missed Scott, and I missed his family, but he'd be back. We, her children, always came back, remember?

I'm not sure that I understood her question correctly, though. She had an inward, preoccupied look on her face, and she did not seem to hear what I said. After I left that evening, Catherine Clark reported the next day, she became quite sad, repeating the words "I miss my children" many times. Catherine reassured her, as I had done, saying that it was hard to have Scott leave, but he would come again.

I wonder, though, if her sadness came from another time and place. I wonder if perhaps it came from the book. After all, I was reading her own words aloud to her, words she had written when she was away from all of us and alone, and thinking and writing about solitude, for weeks at a time on a beach on the island of Captiva. I wonder if, as I read to her, she was suddenly taken back there and began living in that moment of her life again.

It makes sense to me because of the way she floats in time.

I think perhaps as she listened, she floated back to that beach and that winter. She was not hearing the words in her published book, as I was reading them forty-six years after publication. She was instead slipping back into her old self as the writer of those words, a middle-aged woman on a beach, both brilliantly creative and profoundly lonely.

The next day, I was trying to explain to Ben what it was like to read his grandmother's own book aloud to her. I couldn't explain very well, I said to him, but to read her words from a time when she was so articulate, and to have her right there, it was . . .

"It was a real conversation," he said. "I know what you mean." He sounded wiser, older. He surprised me with his understanding, as he does often at this age.

I drove him back to his school at seven on Friday evening, about eight miles each way, because of the possibility that he *might* stay there and go to a dance. He didn't want to commit himself beforehand, he said, because he didn't know if any of his friends would be there. I didn't ask why he hadn't found out who was going earlier in the day, because I thought maybe he was talking about girls, which he would never have admitted.

I agreed to take the chance and drove him to school. When we got there, Ben disappeared for a while inside the building, then came back out to the car. He'd decided to skip it, he said. Only one person from his class, his friend Patrick, was there, "and a bunch of sixth-graders."

"Boys or girls?" I asked as we pulled out, wondering how Patrick would fare all alone.

"I don't know, Mom. They're sixth-graders!" he explained. I thought about that statement as we drove home, but did not come to any conclusions.

We got a few miles down the road toward home when Ben said he thought he'd like to go back to the dance after all, because it would probably be more interesting than just sitting at home all evening. By now it was about seven-thirty, and I knew I would have to pick him up again at school at nine P.M., so I balked. I said I'd picked him up at the school late the night before, because of a field trip, and tonight he'd already changed his mind once, and that was enough. I was sorry.

He said no, *he* was sorry: "I've been kind of demanding lately," and it was fine not to go to the dance.

I felt like a selfish worm, but we were more than halfway home by then, so instead of going back to the dance, I told him how his grandmother always used to try to make us turn around whenever my sister Anne and I drove her to Vermont from Connecticut or to Connecticut from Vermont.

"Take me to Vermont!" she'd plead in West Hartford, heading south. "I want to go to Connecticut!" she would beg as we cruised through White River Junction, the last leg of the journey to Vermont. Back and forth, forth and back. What a time it was!

I said to Ben, "But she's better now, don't you think?"

"I guess so," he said. "She's kind of like a vegetable, though, isn't she?" He sensed my reaction and elaborated carefully, "Kind of a thinking, reading, maybe even intelligent vegetable, I mean?"

"More like a plant!" I protested.

"Yeah," he agreed, "like a . . . pink plant."

I laughed. "She *is* like a pink plant. I often think she's like a rose—sometimes completely droopy and faded and closed up, then she gets watered—and she perks right up!"

"She needs a lot of water," Ben reflected thoughtfully.

I laughed again. "It's true."

But Ben was just warming up. "I mean, we're talking a *monsoon* here, for one little pink rose!"

Okay, okay, I thought, but I couldn't stop chuckling.

We got out of the car together, and Ben grinned over at me. "I want to go to Connecticut!" he said.

Then he ran ahead of me through the snow and the darkness, all the way to the house.

12

February 2001

What power hidden in the winter tree
Can see the captive spirit running free,
Following vault of trunk and leap of limb,
Singing through fountain of the branch a hymn,
Filling through laughter of the twigs in flight
Out to the limitless expanse of light?

—Anne Morrow Lindbergh, from "Winter Tree,"
   The Unicorn and Other Poems

FEBRUARY 5, MONDAY

Yesterday, which would have been my father's ninety-ninth
birthday, I went up the hill in the evening to see my mother. I
brought with me a little photograph of my father as a young
pilot in his aviator suit, cleverly transformed into a jewel-
bedecked brooch by Megan Humphrey, a friend who lives in
Burlington.

Megan works professionally with both the very old and the
very young, and she also makes what I think of as "bejewelry,"

using buttons and beads and rhinestones and ribbons and old photographs and Valentine cupids, all dating from about 1910. I was eager to show this latest effort to my mother. At another time in her life, she would have been amused and charmed.

I was shocked when I arrived at the house. As soon as I came in the door, I saw she was in a different place and in a different chair. Her usual armchair, across the room from the fireplace, was empty. She was in her wheelchair, which the caregivers use only when she is too weak to walk. She seemed to have collapsed in some way. It looked as if she had caved in and given up completely, her head fallen all the way down and resting on the tray in front of her, drooping from her neck like a wilted blossom.

She was not asleep. She was just totally limp and without muscle tone. It was beyond "pink plant," beyond tiredness. It was as if she had relinquished all posture. She looked as slumped and boneless as a rag doll that had been picked up and thrown carelessly in a corner.

I walked over to the wheelchair, very close to her, and crouched down. I tried to show her the photograph-brooch, holding it right up to her face. I had to turn my head sideways to see her eyes.

"Look, Mother! This is such a silly thing, but I love it, don't you? My friend made it and sent it to us, because it's Father's birthday today. He's ninety-nine, of all things!"

There wasn't a sign of life beyond her breathing. I felt pretty stupid. Her eyes, close to mine, were partly open, but the expression in them didn't change. I propped the brooch up against the Beanie Baby robin, which sat in front of her on the tray, and then I sat down next to her. I sat in an unfamiliar chair, in the wrong part of the room. Everything felt strange.

I couldn't get over how loose her body looked, how completely untended by its inhabitant.

On the notepad by the telephone, where the caregivers leave one another updated information about her condition and medications every day, someone had written, "Mrs. L. won't eat. She can't swallow!! What's going on?"

"It's like someone who fell asleep on a bus," Arthur murmured when he came later to help Catherine Clark put her to bed at seven P.M. Catherine, and Sue Gilman before her, found it almost impossible to move my mother from her chair to her bed in this condition. She can't stand up and put her weight on her two feet to use the walker. She can't lift her arms to push up from her chair. We wheeled her into her bedroom, her head hanging.

"Come on, Mrs. L.," coaxed Arthur, bending over her. "Help me out a little. Put your arms around my neck, and I'll get you to bed." He stroked her hand, talked to her, put his face right up into hers. She may have blinked when he did that, just as she may have blinked a moment earlier when I called Land and put the phone up to her ear so he could talk to her. I thought maybe I saw a flicker of response then, too. I wasn't sure.

When I picked up one of her arms and lifted it to curve around Arthur's neck as he bent over her, it dropped back to her side the moment I let go. Finally he just gave her a big bear hug and swung her around slowly and gently until she was in position to be hoisted onto her bed. We propped pillows under all the right places, to discourage pressure sores, and Arthur put the sheepskin ankle cups on her feet for the same purpose. We tucked her in with some of her stuffed animals resting along the side of the bed. I smoothed her forehead, and kissed her, and left the room.

She had had no food, the caregivers told me, and had been able to take only a few ounces of liquid at a time. They had been giving her medicines in water, with an eyedropper, because she did not seem able to swallow well at all. When we laid her head back against the pillow, I could see that her mouth was still full of the yogurt Ann Cason had tried to feed her for supper. Catherine swabbed it out with a warm cloth, and then we left her.

I didn't know about this change, though she has been very tired for the past several days. I skied with Nat in the late afternoon before going up to my mother's. We were on the new trail he made in a short loop around the woods behind the garden, ending up in the field between our house and my mother's.

This morning it was still snowy, with the landscape all blurred and indistinct in the whiteness. All is calm, all is bright, but when I woke up earlier than usual, I could see the light in my mother's window and I realized that I don't want it to go out.

February 6, Tuesday

More and more snow. Two inches an hour, all night long. The power is out, the schools are closed, and Nat went out to plow driveways after starting up the generator at my mother's house.

I am sitting at my kitchen table, with the old Glenwood stove crackling and popping as it warms up the house with wood grown and cut and split and chopped right here on the farm. (Or is it cut and chopped and split? I can never remember. It's easy to see who's responsible for the wood around here!)

I called the Brothers yesterday and have just heard that Jon is already on his way from West Virginia. I don't know if he'll make it in this weather.

1:10 P.M.

Jon and I walked up to the other house to see Mother around eleven-thirty today, he having finally arrived at the nearby Comfort Inn about two-thirty this morning. I'm amazed he got here at all with so many roads impassable and so many airports closed. Being Jon, he made it.

FEBRUARY 8, THURSDAY

My mother died yesterday, Wednesday, February 7, 2001, at about ten A.M. She died just as Jon and I were coming in the door to sit with her for the second day in a row, and just as Land was calling on the phone. I've been told that people sometimes do that. Maybe it's hard to die with your children in the room, so you try to slip away when they are near but not exactly with you. Maybe they pull at the heartstrings too much, make you doubt the wisdom and distract you from the work of your departure. You start to worry about how your dying will affect them, and whether they will be all right afterward. Oh, dear. Should I? Shouldn't I? Are they really ready? Is there anything I forgot to tell them before I go? Do they all have their mittens and their lunch money?

But she went without us, and without apparent pain or struggle. She went quite gracefully, I think. On Tuesday, when Jon and I came to be with her, she sometimes had her eyes open and sometimes was in a deep sleep. When she was awake, her right arm came up often and moved about as if casually waving hello or good-bye, or maybe just conducting her invisible orchestra again, as she has done from her bed in the mornings in recent months.

While I was with her, she would glide her arm along the rail of the hospital bed, sometimes stroking the bedcovers or one of her stuffed animals: the turtle, the ladybug, or her yellow Bumblefish, all of them soft and flat, easy to slide a hand over.

Her arm and hand looked to me like a swan as she wafted them about. The gesture long-necked, elegant, exploring, waving and reaching and touching and retreating, sometimes running over my hand or Jon's or whoever's was there—there were many of us, one after another sitting next to her bed, holding her hand.

Only we weren't really holding her hand. It was more like letting her hand hold ours, or lightly touch and slightly play with the presence of ours, or not. The touch was so light, so playful, hand on hand, a dance of hands. Then hers would drop back slowly toward her neck, curling lightly closed under her chin and resting there. That was where it was when she died.

"She just gave a huge out-breath," Ann Cason told us afterward, "and she was gone."

And so she was. I bent over to kiss her forehead, and it was warm. But she was not breathing—gone.

Behind her head, behind the window and the winter landscape bright with sun and snow, there is a tree, bare-branched. I sat down with my mother's body yesterday morning, next to my brother and the three Buddhist caregivers who had all come to sit with her because they felt instinctively that it was time. I looked past my mother's pale, smooth forehead and cheekbone, past the still, carved oval of her closed eye, and saw the winter tree outside.

And all at once there were birds in it. They were coming and sitting on the branches as I watched. Two chickadees came, flittered, perched, and left. Then two juncos did the same, a pair that jumped playfully from limb to limb and chased each other, changing places, up and down. Last there was a blue jay, who perched solidly on a big lower branch and stayed there. Because of his sudden weight, a clump of snow descended, glittering into crystals as it fell.

Birds came, and left again, and came, and perched, and flew, and fluttered around the branches, just outside my mother's window, just after she died.

There were no birds there the day before. I know because I was sitting in exactly the same place, by my mother's bed, at exactly the same time. I would have seen them. But on Wednesday morning, the moment of her death, the birds came and sat on the branches outside her window, while we were sitting inside in her room.

I'm glad the birds came. In fact, I think I was expecting them.

Epilogue
February 2001

When we knew that Mother was gone, we stayed with her for a while, just sitting by her bed, in her room. Jon and I were there; and several of her caregivers came, one after the other, to sit with her throughout the day and night. We did not move her body for twenty-four hours, though we did report her death right away and her doctor, Tim Thompson, came to certify that she had died. We asked if it would be all right not to have her body taken away for cremation, which was what she had requested, until the next morning, and this delay was permitted.

There was always someone in the room during those twenty-four hours, and there was always a candle burning on the table by her bed. Sometimes the person sitting with her sat alone; sometimes there were two or three of us together. At certain moments the house was completely silent; at others someone would read aloud or sing or say a prayer.

I remember that I recited the 121st Psalm, the one my mother's family always called "The Morrow Prayer," perhaps because it was read at every family funeral and always reminded family members of the Camden Hills in Maine, which could be seen from my grandmother's summer home on the island of North Haven, across Penobscot Bay.

"I will lift up mine eyes unto the hills," I began from memory, and then when I had gotten to the end of the psalm I started over again, because I was pretty sure I had mixed up some of the verses the first time.

After that, or maybe before—time stops for me at birth and death, and I lose track of things—I also read aloud a prayer of St. Augustine. The prayer had been written out in my mother's handwriting on a piece of paper that was folded and tucked inside the cover of a pocket-sized edition of the Book of Common Prayer that was sitting on her bedside table. On the paper she had marked in pencil, neatly, "To be read at A.M.L.'s death."

It did not say "to be read at my funeral," although the prayer was indeed read again at the service, ten days later, when all the family came from all over the world and we gathered for a "Celebration of the Life of Anne Morrow Lindbergh" in the Congregational Church in Peacham, Vermont, where my mother had been to services many times over the years.

At her own service we had all the relatives and friends and neighbors from near and far who were able to get to the church on that snowy February morning, and we included all her favorite hymns and prayers, a few special songs and readings by people from the local community who had known and loved her, and even a Rilke poem, "The Swan," read by poet and Vermont resident Galway Kinnell, from a book of translations he had recently done with Hannah Liebmann.

But on this day, the day our mother died, I remembered that Land had told me over the phone to look in her prayer book for suggestions as to what she wanted done after her death. When I looked, I found this prayer, and it seemed to me that she wanted it to be read right away, so I read it.

> *O Thou God Omnipotent, who so carest for every one of us as if thou*
> *carest for him alone, and so for all, as if all were one; Blessed is*
> *the man who loveth thee, and his friend in Thee and his enemy for thee.*
> *For he only loses none dear to him, for whom all are dear in Him who*
> *cannot be lost. And who is that but our God, the God that made heaven*
> *and earth, and filleth them, even by filling them creating them. And*
> *Thy law is truth, and truth is Thyself. I behold how some things pass*
> *away that others may replace them, but Thou dost never depart, O God,*
> *my Father, supremely good, Beauty of all things Beautiful. To Thee I*
> *will entrust whatsoever I have received from Thee, so shall I lose*
> *nothing. Thou madest me for Thyself, and my heart is restless until it*
> *repose in Thee.*

Nat came up to the house after a while and joined us in my mother's room. I asked if he'd like to read something out loud, and he said he would. He chose one of my mother's poems, "Testament," from *The Unicorn and Other Poems.*

"Testament" is not a poem I have often chosen to read aloud myself lately, and especially not during the past few years with my mother, because it tends to make me cry.

When I read this poem the tears come in floods, even when I think that I am in full control of my emotions and not vulnerable to tears because, I imagine, the moment is too public, too busy, or too astonishing. I find myself overwhelmed by a sharp and sudden grief, whose arrival is as unexpected as the actual moment of my mother's death, something else that I didn't really believe was going to happen, until it did.

Nat always has had good instincts, though. He knew that on this particular bright winter morning, the poem he read was the right choice for us all.

Testament
But how can I live without you?—she cried.

I left all world to you when I died:
Beauty of earth and air and sea;
Leap of a swallow or a tree;
Kiss of rain and wind's embrace;
Passion of storm and winter's face;
Touch of feather, flower and stone;
Chiselled line of branch of bone;
Flight of stars, night's caravan;
Song of crickets—and of man—
All these I put in my testament,
All these I bequeathed to you when I went.

But how can I see them without your eyes
Or touch them without your hand?

How can I hear them without your ear,
Without your heart, understand?

These too, these too
I leave to you!

Printed in the United States
By Bookmasters